MAR -- 2009

W9-DIH-175

362.4 PEO

People with disabilities /

PALM BEACH COUNTY
LIBRARY SYSTEM
3650 SUMMIT BLVD.
WEST PALM BEACH, FLORIDA 33406

THE
HISTORY
OF
ISSUES

People with Disabilities

Other Books in the History of Issues Series

THE
HISTORY
OF
ISSUES

People with Disabilities

Dawn Laney, Book Editor

GREENHAVEN PRESS
A part of Gale, Cengage Learning

GALE
CENGAGE Learning·

Detroit • New York • San Francisco • New Haven, Conn • Waterville, Maine • London

Christine Nasso, *Publisher*
Elizabeth Des Chenes, *Managing Editor*

© 2008 Greenhaven Press, a part of Gale, Cengage Learning

Gale and Greenhaven Press are registered trademarks used herein under license.

For more information, contact:
Greenhaven Press
27500 Drake Rd.
Farmington Hills, MI 48331-3535
Or you can visit our Internet site at gale.cengage.com

ALL RIGHTS RESERVED.
No part of this work covered by the copyright herein may be reproduced, transmitted, stored, or used in any form or by any means graphic, electronic, or mechanical, including but not limited to photocopying, recording, scanning, digitizing, taping, Web distribution, information networks, or information storage and retrieval systems, except as permitted under Section 107 or 108 of the 1976 United States Copyright Act, without the prior written permission of the publisher.

For product information and technology assistance, contact us at

Gale Customer Support, 1-800-877-4253
For permission to use material from this text or product, submit all requests online at
www.cengage.com/permissions

Further permissions questions can be emailed to permissionrequest@cengage.com

Articles in Greenhaven Press anthologies are often edited for length to meet page requirements. In addition, original titles of these works are changed to clearly present the main thesis and to explicitly indicate the author's opinion. Every effort is made to ensure that Greenhaven Press accurately reflects the original intent of the authors. Every effort has been made to trace the owners of copyrighted material.

Cover image copyright Vadim Kozlovsky, 2008. Used under license from Shutterstock.com.

LIBRARY OF CONGRESS CATALOGING-IN-PUBLICATION DATA

People with disabilities / Dawn Laney, book editor.
 p. cm. -- (History of issues)
 Includes bibliographical references and index.
 ISBN-13: 978-0-7377-3972-5 (hardcover)
 1. People with disabilities--United States. 2. People with disabilities--United States --Education. I. Laney, Dawn.
 HV1553.P435 2008
 362.40973--dc22

 2008020216

Printed in the United States of America
1 2 3 4 5 6 7 12 11 10 09 08

Contents

Chapter 2: Issues Faced by People with Disabilities

Chapter 3: Education for People with Disabilities

Chapter 4: The Impact of Technological Advances on the Disabled

Foreword

In the 1940s, at the height of the Holocaust, Jews struggled to create a nation of their own in Palestine, a region of the Middle East that at the time was controlled by Britain. The British had placed limits on Jewish immigration to Palestine, hampering efforts to provide refuge to Jews fleeing the Holocaust. In response to this and other British policies, an underground Jewish resistance group called Irgun began carrying out terrorist attacks against British targets in Palestine, including immigration, intelligence, and police offices. Most famously, the group bombed the King David Hotel in Jerusalem, the site of a British military headquarters. Although the British were warned well in advance of the attack, they failed to evacuate the building. As a result, ninety-one people were killed (including fifteen Jews) and forty-five were injured.

Early in the twentieth century, Ireland, which had long been under British rule, was split into two countries. The south, populated mostly by Catholics, eventually achieved independence and became the Republic of Ireland. Northern Ireland, mostly Protestant, remained under British control. Catholics in both the north and south opposed British control of the north, and the Irish Republican Army (IRA) sought unification of Ireland as an independent nation. In 1969, the IRA split into two factions. A new radical wing, the Provisional IRA, was created and soon undertook numerous terrorist bombings and killings throughout Northern Ireland, the Republic of Ireland, and even in England. One of its most notorious attacks was the 1974 bombing of a Birmingham, England, bar that killed nineteen people.

In the mid-1990s, an Islamic terrorist group called al Qaeda began carrying out terrorist attacks against American targets overseas. In communications to the media, the organization listed several complaints against the United States. It generally opposed all U.S. involvement and presence in the Middle East. It particularly objected to the presence of U.S. troops in Saudi Arabia, which is the home of several Islamic holy sites. And it strongly condemned the United States for supporting the nation of Israel, which it claimed was an oppressor of Muslims. In 1998 al Qaeda's leaders issued a fatwa (a religious legal statement) calling for Muslims to kill Americans. Al Qaeda acted on this order many times—most memorably on September 11, 2001, when it attacked the World Trade Center and the Pentagon, killing nearly three thousand people.

These three groups—Irgun, the Provisional IRA, and al Qaeda—have achieved varied results. Irgun's terror campaign contributed to Britain's decision to pull out of Palestine and to support the creation of Israel in 1948. The Provisional IRA's tactics kept pressure on the British, but they also alienated many would-be supporters of independence for Northern Ireland. Al Qaeda's attacks provoked a strong U.S. military response but did not lessen America's involvement in the Middle East nor weaken its support of Israel. Despite these different results, the means and goals of these groups were similar. Although they emerged in different parts of the world during different eras and in support of different causes, all three had one thing in common: They all used clandestine violence to undermine a government they deemed oppressive or illegitimate.

The destruction of oppressive governments is not the only goal of terrorism. For example, terror is also used to minimize dissent in totalitarian regimes and to promote extreme ideologies. However, throughout history the motivations of terrorists have been remarkably similar, proving the old adage that "the more things change, the more they remain the same." Arguments for and against terrorism thus boil down to the same set of universal arguments regardless of the age: Some argue that terrorism is justified to change (or, in the case of state terror, to maintain) the prevailing political order; others respond that terrorism is inhumane and unacceptable under any circumstances. These basic views transcend time and place.

Similar fundamental arguments apply to other controversial social issues. For instance, arguments over the death penalty have always featured competing views of justice. Scholars cite biblical texts to claim that a person who takes a life must forfeit his or her life, while others cite religious doctrine to support their view that only God can take a human life. These arguments have remained essentially the same throughout the centuries. Likewise, the debate over euthanasia has persisted throughout the history of Western civilization. Supporters argue that it is compassionate to end the suffering of the dying by hastening their impending death; opponents insist that it is society's duty to make the dying as comfortable as possible as death takes its natural course.

Greenhaven Press's *The History of Issues* series illustrates this constancy of arguments surrounding major social issues. Each volume in the series focuses on one issue—including terrorism, the death penalty, and euthanasia—and examines how the debates have both evolved and remained essentially the same over the years. Primary documents such as newspaper articles, speeches, and government reports illuminate historical developments and offer perspectives from throughout history. Secondary sources provide overviews and commentaries from a more contemporary perspective. An introduction begins each anthology and supplies essential context and background. An annotated table of contents, chronology, and index allow for easy reference, and a bibliography and list of organizations to contact point to additional sources of information on the book's topic. With these features, *The History of Issues* series permits readers to glimpse both the historical and contemporary dimensions of humanity's most pressing and controversial social issues.

Introduction

Today's increased opportunities for people with disabilities have been made possible through the advocacy of disabled people and organizations, legislative changes over the past thirty years, an increased understanding of the need for individualized education plans, and technological innovations. The current positive perspective in the United States on people with disabilities represents an evolution of the rights and opportunities of disabled persons from ancient to modern times.

Treatment of People with Disabilities in Ancient Times

The earliest evidence of a societal approach to people with disabilities appeared in the Paleolithic era. In these early human societies, individual tribes or groups traveled from place to place hunting and gathering food and supplies. In these communities, children who were born prematurely or with physical birth defects were often killed or left to die soon after birth. These practices were the result of scarce food resources, constant external threats to survival, and the community's need to curb physical limitations.

Over hundreds of years, the number of hunter-gather communities decreased and the number of sedentary and established communities increased. One of the largest and most advanced ancient societies that developed is that of the ancient Greeks, from 750 BC–146 BC. The predominant Greek custom and legislation at the time stated that individuals who were weak or disabled at birth were not viable and recommended passively killing newborns by leaving them outdoors to die—a practice known as exposure—or actively killing these infants. An integral part of this practice was the ancient Greek belief that the physical appearance of an individual mirrored their societal worth and goodness. Inhabitants of ancient Sparta conducted controlled matings and killed disabled infants in order to pursue a strong, physically attractive nation. As professor John A. Scott reports in a 1915 *Chicago Daily Tribune* article, "Whenever a child, male or female, was born to Spartan parents . . . it had no legal standing in the state until its physical fitness had been passed upon by certain constituted officials. This body of men, made up of the leaders in the community, determined whether it should live or die." Beyond the Spartans, early Greek and Roman laws gave fathers the power to decide if their child should live or die.

One of the first groups to condemn the killing of disabled or unwanted children was the early Christian church. Christian philosophy increased in popularity and by the fourth century AD, the Roman emperor Constantine, a Christian convert, proclaimed the slaying of a child by the child's father to be a crime. This condemnation of the direct killing of the disabled continued through the Middle Ages and into the twentieth century; however, exposure or passive death were still considered options. Exposure or abandonment continued in part because even in Christian-dominated societies children born with physical defects or behavioral abnormalities were often viewed as evil, the result of parental sin, or the product of supernatural forces. In his book *Inventing the Feeble Mind: A History of Mental Retardation in the United States*, James Trent notes, "To have a defective in the family was to be associated with vice, immorality, failure, bad blood, and stupidity."

The Rise of Institutions

In 1863 the first institutions for the care of the physically and mentally disabled were created in the United States. The institutions were the first attempt by the government to take public responsibility for the disabled by providing care and education. Institutions were also a response to the industrial revolution of the late eighteenth and early nineteenth centuries, when work was concentrated in factories rather than homes and farms. Factory work required precise mechanical movements of the body repeated in quick succession, and the physically and mentally disabled were seen as less able to do the required tasks. A decreased ability for the disabled to find work resulted in an increased need for assistance in food, housing, and learning. When a disabled child was born, doctors, religious advisers, and family members would recommend placing them in institutions for education and proper care. The theory was that disabled people were best segregated from society and would receive more appropriate care and education in an institution than with their family and community. Institutions became a place to isolate and contain the disabled.

The removal of disabled persons from local communities decreased the average person's familiarity with the disabled. In the early twentieth century, there were few individuals willing to refute a popular social theory that stated the mentally retarded posed a threat to society as their weak powers of reasoning made them more likely than others to indulge in criminal activity or immoral sexual behavior. In addition, eugenic principles, the belief that specially selected matings of some and forced sterilization of others will improve the human race, rose from doctors and scientists and became accepted practice. Laws were made in order to recommend sterilization of the disabled, "mentally feeble," or unfit. The movements recommended no medical intervention to treat newborns with birth defects. This approach was considered more humane as the life of a disabled child was considered one of pain and suffering. As one 1915 journalist states, "Death will be nature's means of righting its mistake."

Eugenic principles led to the extermination programs of Nazi Germany and leader Adolf Hitler. In Nazi Germany, the push for planned matings to attain what Hitler considered the perfect race was combined with programs of murder to remove the "undesirables" from the reproductive gene pool. In

1939, Hitler ordered the killing of the sick and disabled to eliminate "life unworthy of life." When society took a long hard look at the programs that represented the twentieth-century eugenic approach to the disabled, most recoiled in horror from their previously held principles.

Revamping Policies Toward Persons with Disabilities

After rejecting the eugenic principles, U.S. policy makers reviewed all of the standard practices related to the disabled. They examined the policy of institutionalization. Investigations into institutions found squalor and substandard care. In many cases the facilities were overcrowded, understaffed, and unclean. In addition, there were no education programs in most institutions. In 1967 a visitor to one California state-run hospital observed, as reported by Trent, "wards of naked adults sleeping on cement floors often in their own excrement or wandering in open dayrooms." As the negative information on the institutions emerged, parents reacted. They took a lead role in developing a policy of deinstitutionalization and rejected the secrecy and guilt surrounding having children with disabilities. The families of disabled persons fought for government assistance, access to education, community programs, and family care.

In addition, advocates staged protests and rallies to lobby for improved access to public buildings and facilities, education, and legal rights. In the late 1940s and 1950s, disability support groups, organizations, and associations such as The Association for Retarded Children of the United States (now called The ARC) were formed to bring individuals with disabilities and their families together to educate the public, advocate for their rights, and support each other. In 1951 the Institute of Rehabilitation Medicine at New York University Medical Center began work on innovations and adaptive aids for individuals with disabilities to help them live independently. In the late 1950s and early 1960s, several athletic competitions such as the National Wheelchair Games were organized to bring the disabled together in competition and camaraderie. Over time, exposure to the disabled and their advocates introduced the general public to the concept that disabled people could live outside the institution and lead productive lives. In 1961, a presidential committee was formed to develop solutions to the needs of individuals with disabilities and their desire to be integrated into the community. In the 1970s, thousands of mentally disabled individuals were deinstitutionalized and became integrated into their communities, public schools, and workplaces. In 1977, a law was passed that required the development of individualized education plans for individuals with disabilities. The Americans with Disabilities Act, comprehensive federal civil rights law that prohibits discrimination on the basis of disability, was passed in 1990. Each of these pieces of legislature and advocacy provided more opportunities for individuals with disabilities. By the early twenty-first century, the opportunities available for disabled persons have moved well beyond the darkest beginnings of infanticide into widespread acceptance and integration in society.

CHAPTER 1

Disability in Modern Times

Chapter Preface

Modern society's generally receptive attitude toward people with disabilities is a direct result of the disability rights movement. In this movement, individuals with disabilities, their families, and other advocates challenged long-held stereotypes and surmounted societal barriers. The main goals of the movement were to refute the beliefs that people with physical or mental challenges are unable to hold jobs or function independently and to gain increased access to society. From the organized protests in 1935 by the League for the Physically Handicapped against the government-run Works Progress Administration (WPA) that had denied them jobs to protests against the practice of testing fetuses for disabilities prior to birth, members of the disability rights movement have garnered a strong voice to promote themselves, their perspectives, and their abilities.

An excellent example of the progress of the organized disability rights movement is that of Ed Roberts, an activist in the 1960s and 1970s. At age fourteen Roberts contracted polio and spent the rest of his adolescence in hospitals attached to devices that helped him breathe. During the first days of his illness, his mother asked the doctor whether he would live or die. The doctor told his mother, "You should hope he dies, because if he lives, he'll be no more than a vegetable for the rest of his life." Thus began Roberts's fight against low expectations. Despite his physical limitations, he graduated from high school and applied for admission to college. The college of his choice rejected his application based on its concerns that he would be unable to function independently enough to complete his studies. Roberts fought against this stereotype and then, after winning that battle, continued to fight for reduced barriers to independent living and for accessibility for all disabled individuals.

His personal crusade expanded to include other disability rights issues and he became one of the founders of the disability rights movement. As he stated in a 1970s victory speech in San Francisco, "We, who are considered the weakest, the most helpless people in our society, are the strongest, and will not tolerate segregation, will not tolerate a society which sees us as less than whole people. . . . We will together, with our friends, will reshape the image that this society has of us." The following chapter provides a brief survey of the struggles that disability rights groups have overcome in seeking opportunities for the disabled in an effort to change society's general perception of those individuals.

Infants with Disabilities Should Not Receive Lifesaving Treatment

Chicago Daily Tribune

In 1915 United States physicians such as Dr. H.J. Haiselden advocated allowing physically or mentally disabled newborns to die rather than actively saving them through surgery or other medical treatment. This attitude reflects the rise of eugenic principles in the first part of the twentieth century that strove to "improve" the human race by allowing only the fit to survive into adulthood. The following selection by the staff writers of the Chicago Daily Tribune *examines the chief physician and mother's decision to allow an infant with disabilities to die.*

Nature has blundered at the German-American hospital, 810 Divorsey Parkway [in Chicago]. The error is a malformed baby, which, if it lived, would grow to be a mental, and perhaps a moral defective. Death will be nature's means of righting its mistake.

Dr. H. J. Haiselden, chief of the hospital staff, will allow the baby to die. He will not aid or hasten nature toward the inevitable fatality. His role is that of onlooker.

Parental Consent

The baby was born on Friday [November 12, 1915]. A simple surgical operation at birth would have insured its life. The same simple operation now would assure life [of] the infant. But the surgeon declines to perform this operation. The baby's mother is satisfied. She has given her consent to the infant's death, which is expected to occur in forty-eight hours.

The baby is the son of Allen and Mrs. Ann Bollinger of 2013 Fletcher street. Mr. Bollinger is repair foreman at the

Chicago Daily Tribune, "Dr. Haiselden and the Bollinger Baby," November 17, 1915.

Lincoln Avenue car barns at Sheffield avenue. He and his wife have three other children—Ida, aged 6; Gilbert, 4, and Margaret, 3, all fine, healthy children. The last baby—the baby doomed to die—was born after his mother had been seriously ill with typhoid fever. The doctor thinks this fact accounts for his deformity.

Dr. Haiselden boldly champions the right of physicians to snuff out the lives of babies born deformed or with the stigma of imbecility upon them. He not only thinks this is the right of physicians, but a duty they owe to the future. He believes in upbuilding the race by allowing only the fit to survive.

Physician Advocates Eugenic Principles

Dr. Haiselden stands at the edge of a problem big with the fate of humanity and the future. He comes out openly and advocates death for defective children, sterilization of imbeciles, and euthanasia for the hopelessly sick or insane.

"I have no doubt I shall be called a cold blooded murderer for allowing this baby to die," said Dr. Haiselden. "I am prepared for bitter criticism. But its death is a question between me and my conscience. I would not kill the infant. I would not administer poison or take its life by any active surgical means. I shall merely stand by passively and let it die. I will let nature complete its bungled job."

While Dr. Haiselden talked, a nurse brought in a bundle and laid it on a couch. The doctor turned back the wrappings. A pink bit of humanity lay upon the white cloth. Its blue eyes were wide open. Its hair was brown and silky. It dug at its face with little fists. It cried lustily as it drew up chubby legs and kicked out. It seemed quite vigorously informed with life.

But one noted there were deformities, and the physician explained further the results of an examination which showed the infant inevitably would be a defective.

Not Afraid of the Law

"Are you not afraid of the law if you let this baby die?" Dr. Haiselden was asked.

"No," he replied. "I am doing what I believe right. I expect censure, but I believe my course will be approved by tens of thousands of thinking men and women. I do not court prosecution. But I am not afraid of it. If there is any law to force a physician to perform an operation when his conscience tells him that operation would be morally wrong, then let them bring the law to bear. To compel a surgeon to perform such an operation against his will would be like forcing a man to be a Mohammedan (Muslim) who wished to be a Methodist.

"I knew of no law to which I might possibly be held amenable, unless it be that against criminal neglect. I am sure no jury of sane men would convict me of allowing a child to die who would be a burden to himself and to the community if permitted to live."

Many Allowed to Die

"Do physicians in secret permit deformed and defective children to die a-borning [while being born] often?" he was asked.

"Not infrequently," Dr. Haiselden replied. "Many a child marked plainly as an id[i]ot or badly deformed has been allowed to die by not tieing the umbilical cord. If the cord, which must be severed at birth, is not tied immediately after, the infant will die of loss of blood. I do not mean to say that children are permitted often to die by their physicians. But such deaths are not infrequent.

"Instead of struggling to save deformed children and those marked plainly for insanity and uselessness," the surgeon continued, "physicians should have only the fit. I have thought over this problem for years.

"There are no defectives among the Japanese. The surgeons of Nippon often fail to tie the umbilical cord. As a result, the Japanese are a wonderfully vigorous race deservedly coming into world prominence.

"I am an advocate of sterilization not only of infants of defective parents, but of criminals and the insane. Infant mortality is unfortunately low in families of epileptics, the partially insane, and those of criminal tendencies."

"Do you number criminals among the insane?"

"They are abnormal. However, I should not advocate their being executed, except in capital cases. I would have all criminals sterilized by law."

City Full of Defectives

"Chicago is full of defectives," Dr. Haiselden concluded. "The average physician today saves imbeciles at birth. This adds to the crime waves of the city's future. There will be a great awakening some day which will result in the enactment of laws providing for the sterilization of the criminal and the lunatic, and possibly for the painless death of the hopelessly insane."

Dr. Haiselden is a graduate of the Chicago medical department of the University of Illinois. He resided at the German hospital for three and a half years, where he was under the famous Dr. Christian Fenger.

Institutions Offer Substandard Care for People with Disabilities

Gordon Zahn

In the early and mid-twentieth century, parents were often advised to put their mentally retarded or disabled children into residential care so that they could be taught and cared for appropriately. In the following viewpoint, American sociologist Gordon Zahn uses the example of the Rosewood State Training School in Maryland to explain the often substandard and unsanitary conditions available to the disabled. Zahn explains that Rosewood failed to educate higher-functioning children and to provide adequate care for low-functioning children.

"All hope abandon, ye who enter here" is the inscription fashioned by Dante [Alighieri] for the gates of Hell [in the epic poem *The Divine Comedy*. It was in no burst of poetic fancy that the sign, "Rosewood—No Thoroughfare," was placed at the foot of the lane leading to the "training school" for the mentally deficient of Maryland; yet, that inscription is every bit as fitting as Dante's. Escape or death are virtually the only ways out for the unfortunate child committed there. Rosewood State Training School, as we ... witnessed for almost three full years, is strictly a one way, dead-end street.

Rosewood Fails

About one-fourth of the patient body at Rosewood consists of custodial cases. Most of these are individuals with mentality of infant level or lower. All any institution could do for them is to provide adequate care and reasonably pleasant surround-

Gordon Zahn, "Abandon Hope," *The Catholic Worker*, vol. 13, no. 8, October 1946, pp. 1, 4, 6.

ings. However, Rosewood fails even in this respect. Instead these unfortunates are herded together into huge basement "playrooms"; the total effect of the smell, sight and sounds of Rosewood's Hill Cottage can be guaranteed to produce revulsion and often nausea into anyone viewing it for the first time. Insofar as these patients are concerned, the entire fault for the state of affairs lies with the stinginess of the Maryland Legislature; even if the Rosewood administration wished to improve their lot, no funds would be available for this purpose.

The Real Tragedy

The real tragedy of Rosewood lies . . . in the inadequate provisions for the care and *eventual return to Society* of those boys and girls of the higher mental levels. In name, and in name only, Rosewood is a training school. This should imply that a child placed there would be given the benefits of an adequate program of education, recreation and social guidance: the first to develop his mental abilities to their maximum; the second to promote physical and mental health and build a sense of teamwork and sportsmanship; the last to assist him to readjust himself properly to a Society against which he had previously rebelled. On all counts Rosewood fails miserably—and here the fault lies principally in the institution itself and in the individuals to which these responsibilities have been entrusted!

The Only Exit

The goal of every admission to Rosewood (except those which are obviously custodial in nature) should be parole. Yet in those three years the only paroles of Rosewood resulted from successful "escapes" or from actual court actions instituted by interested parties. Since the great majority of children there are not blessed with sufficiently interested parties, the latter cases were few indeed. Is it not a sad commentary on the merits of Rosewood as a training school that the only exit routes were to run away or to force a way out by legal procedure.

The System Fails

Wherein the failing? First, in a totally inadequate educational program. These children failed intellectually in all of their regular or special public school classes. Still we find the Rosewood program based on the same type of subjects with little or no attention given to individual interests or capabilities. Granting that these general subjects are a valuable foundation; is it not unwise to place full stress on them to the detriment or elimination of other training in which the child would find more value? Rosewood can be complimented on its efforts to gain an accurate survey of each patient by employing an extensive variety of psychological tests and measurements. But of what possible worth is an elaborate psychological study of a patient who shows mechanical abilities and interests if the "school" provides no facilities whatsoever for the development of such interests and abilities into worthwhile occupational training? It is futile to attempt the training of mentally limited patients on a group basis. Each of them must be accepted as an individual problem with the training and education planned to meet his individual needs and capabilities.

Rosewood is utterly unfit to do such a job. In the first place, it again lacks the facilities. It is almost inconceivable that the State of Maryland would knowingly operate such an institution without providing equipment for shop work and other mechanical training. Unfortunately, however, even if this were not the case, the Rosewood teaching personnel lacks the imagination, the inspiration and the ability to adapt themselves to the needs of each individual pupil. The best measure of the value of any training school lies in the number of patients it succeeds in salvaging for Society; judged according to this standard the Rosewood educational program is a total failure.

The lack of an adequate recreational program has already been discussed in detail. Suffice it to say, then, that so long as this great need is not met, Rosewood will have little success in its efforts to convert its patients—especially those committed because of delinquent trends—into citizens of promise.

Responsibility

One factor in a child's development which should be given some consideration here, since it has great bearing on ultimate parole eligibility, is spiritual and moral training. Even though it is a State institution, the Church should be awakened to its responsibilities to these children. Mass is said at Rosewood once a *month*: beyond that the only religious guidance provided for the Catholic children is a Sunday school program conducted by seminarians. (It required the initiative of two of our men to train some of the Rosewood boys as Mass-servers). How can we expect these children to return to a normal life, regular in the practice of their religion, if the Church is so lax in making the Sacraments available to them in the formative years of their training? Other institutions are able to have weekly Sunday Masses for their patients; certainly the clergy of Maryland should make every effort to do the same. If it is the Catholic's obligation to attend weekly Mass, it is certainly the clergy's duty to bring that weekly Mass to those institutionalized Catholics who are not free to meet their obligations. Surely there would be immeasurable value to the spiritual and moral development of the Rosewood patients in the regular, and much more frequent, practice of their Catholic faith.

Individualized education, recreational outlets, character moulding, etc., would be to little avail without a well-planned and efficiently handled program of social guidance. Therefore, the main responsibility for successful paroles (or for the lack of them) lies with the job done by the social worker.

No Effort Made

For quite some time Rosewood had no social worker—and when one was finally added to the staff, there was no great indication of competence or of the slightest understanding of the true scope of the duties associated with the position. Absolutely no effort was made by this individual to learn to know the patients on a friendly, personal basis. Instead full emphasis was placed on the prominence of her status in the institution's professional clique.

The social worker of an institution such as Rosewood has a great opportunity. By making it a point to meet *and know* each patient, his background, the events leading to his committment [sic] and so on such an official could—in cooperation with the staff psychologist—map out the training program for each patient on an individual basis. Then, by establishing and maintaining a friendly rapport with the patient, the social worker could assist him by guiding him through his problems at the school. And, finally, when the patient advances to parole, the social worker must continue that personal friendship and maintain an occasional but regular follow-up—*again as a personal friend, not as a policeman checking up*—to help the "graduate" through problems outside, lest failure and disillusionment drive him back to the social habits that originally caused his rejection by Society.

This is a mighty task—almost too great perhaps for any one person. But it is one which certainly cannot be accomplished by sitting at a desk or conferring endlessly with other staff members, compiling social summaries that could be put together by an ordinary stenographer. Nor can there be any hope for success if the individual holding the job treats the patients as "untouchables" or hopeless reprobates.

Dissension

Rosewood fails on all three scores—education, recreation, social guidance—primarily because it does not have the personnel big enough for these jobs. The best of facilities would be worthless in an institution in which the professional staff—doctors, nurses, teachers, social workers, and on down the line—are torn by factional jealousies agitated by vicious gossip and rumormongering. Educated professional people who cannot adjust themselves to each other within their sheltered environment are obviously not qualified to assume responsibility for the adjustment of these unfortunate children to an unfamiliar and unfriendly Society. . . .

Remedy

Such criticism carries with it the obligation to suggest remedial action.

The first—and most obvious—step is to eradicate incompetence wherever it may be found. Until this is done, no corrective effort at improvement can succeed. And this is not to be limited to the institution personnel. If the present members of the Board of Visitors are unwilling or find themselves unable to do a reasonably effective job of protecting the patients and the public against the excesses of an otherwise all-powerful administration, they should resign and turn the job over to others who would take a sincere interest in so important a task.

Then, once Rosewood's house is in order, full publicity must be given to the needs of the institution and its patients. Instead of "sitting tight" on a disgusting situation, the administrative staff and Dr. Preston's Board of Mental Hygiene should expose and advertise the handicaps placed upon them by a niggardly and penny-pinching legislature. We who have listened long and often to their complaints cannot reconcile them with an officially-stated policy of "no bombshells." These people are sitting on a bombshell potent enough to shake action out of the most miserly legislature. For the "bombshell" is the fact that the State of Maryland is responsible for a grave moral crime, the neglect and maltreatment of helpless children. Once the electorate of Maryland is made aware of the crime that has been perpetrated in its name, it will react against those who are guilty of the raw deal these children have been getting *and are still getting!*

The people of Maryland have the right and the Christian duty to demand full investigations to learn who is accountable for this situation. Only if they act can there be hope that Rosewood may yet become a thoroughfare of promise.

Parents Fight for Increased Rights for People with Disabilities

Margaret McDonald

In the 1950s parents began to question the status quo that suggested they should place their disabled children in institutions and continue on with their lives. Parents refuted the idea that it was socially unacceptable to mention the mentally retarded and disabled and rejected the idea that they should feel ashamed and guilty to have a disabled child. Through grassroots funding from friends, family, and local organizations, parents worked on a local level to develop schools, training programs, and vocational workshops. In this selection, Margaret McDonald charts the progress of one family that rejected recommendations to institutionalize their children and instead focused on making life better for disabled children in their community. Margaret McDonald wrote this article in 1956 for The Rotarian, *a publication of the Rotary service club organization.*

It would have been easier, really, for Morley and Lucy Hudson if their little Lucy had died.

Death is heartbreaking, but it is also inevitable and final, and the sorrow it brings is universally understood and respected.

But when this fine couple—this Rotary couple, as you would call them—found that their pretty little girl would never develop mentally, they felt that their heartache was unique, and they soon discovered that few can fathom the grief of those whose loved ones are condemned to the land of the living dead.

It was many months before this normally jolly businessman of Shreveport, Louisiana, learned to live with the knowl-

Margaret McDonald, "Because a Father Cared," *The Rotarian*, November 1956.

edge that his child probably will spend the rest of her allotted span on earth in the desolate strata of existence which hope seldom reaches and promise rarely brightens.

Because Morley Hudson became convinced that this tragedy had befallen his family for a purpose, the parents of mentally retarded children throughout Louisiana and in several adjoining States now can face the future with serenity and, in many instances, with hope as well.

Personal Tragedy Transformed into a Mission

Rotarian Hudson's personal tragedy served as the springboard for the organization of the Caddo-Bossier Association for Mentally Retarded Children. It also proved the stimulant for the almost unbelievable development of the Louisiana Association for Retarded Children. From it, too, have sprung similar organizations in Texas, Arkansas, and Mississippi.

The wave of activity by parents of mentally retarded children in all sections of the U.S.A., some of which undoubtedly was inspired by the action of Louisiana parents, is a social phenomenon almost without precedence in any country.

Morley Hudson feels his experience was typical of that of other parents of mentally retarded or brain-injured children. When he was first informed of his daughter's affliction, he felt an acute sense of guilt and something akin to shame.

"I remember wondering what I had done to deserve this terrible punishment," he says. "I wondered of what sin I had been guilty that this should happen to me. I felt that life had been unfair to me."

A Heartbreaking Tragedy

At birth, little Lucy was a completely normal infant. At age 14 months she suffered an attack of scarlet fever and encephalitis which damaged her brain and left her in what medical and psychiatric experts term the "vegetative" state.

After months of treatment Lucy still recognized no one, showed no emotions, and was totally disinterested in her surroundings. Her arms and legs, which had been drawn up in a spastic position, gradually relaxed, but in six months' time no other sign of her recovery manifested itself.

In January, 1953, the child was taken to a children's hospital in Chicago where her parents were informed that she probably would spend the rest of her life in the vegetative state. Mr. and Mrs. Hudson were advised to place her in a custodial home to spare further heartache for themselves and additional difficulties for their older daughter, Nancy, now 8.

Limited Options

"The shock of receiving news like that is something no one can understand unless he has experienced it," Rotarian Hudson maintains. "We began inspecting custodial homes, but they all seemed so bleak we couldn't bear to leave a 2-year-old child in any of them. Then we heard of a lovely, homelike place in Texas, so we took Lucy there."

Some eight months later the Hudsons learned of a new type of treatment which had proved effective in treating acute encephalitis cases on the West Coast. Lucy was taken to California in August, 1953, but here further grief awaited them. They were told that the child was, for all practical purposes, blind and deaf as well as mentally retarded.

Until about a year ago Lucy remained at the California hospital, where she eventually learned to sit up, to chew solid foods, and to crawl about to some extent. Her mental development, however, lagged far behind her physical advances.

Learning About Mental Retardation

"All those long, lonely months I had been doing a lot of thinking and self-probing," Morley Hudson recalls. "I began to understand that I must stop asking myself *why* this had happened to me and must begin thinking in terms of *how* I could use my personal tragedy to the greater glory of God and *what* I could do to ensure this unfortunate child of mine a life of happiness and usefulness. Once I had adopted this line of thinking, the way became clear to me."

Morley began reading all available information on mental retardation. He learned that 3 percent of the world's population is mentally retarded and that the odds are one in 30 that every family will be stricken with one mentally retarded member. In fact, the chances are four times greater that someone in every family will be mentally retarded than that someone will be killed in an automobile accident.

He learned, too, that mental retardation is nine times more prevalent than cerebral palsy and ten times more crippling than polio. According to best information, mentally retarded persons exceed accumulated totals of all other handicapped persons combined, speaking numerically. Even more comforting from a personal standpoint was the discovery that medical experts consider mental retardation as accidental as a broken leg and are convinced that it is not hereditary.

Joining Together to Combat Stereotypes

Armed with this information, Morley set about to interest others in the problem of mentally retarded children and to dispel the old wives' tales concerning its causes. He first attempted to call forth other parents of mentally retarded children, many of whom kept their youngsters hidden as a result of combined guilt-shame reactions. Some, when approached, even denied having mentally retarded children, while others refused to discuss the matter from acknowledged embarrassment and fear of public ridicule. It was only after Hudson aired the problem publicly, through a newspaper interview, that others decided they, too, would align themselves with him in an effort to work for the betterment of their children.

On Sunday, January 24, 1954, a group of 14 parents met at the home of one couple to seek reassurance from each other and to discuss ways of obtaining help for their children. After six successive Sunday-night meetings ... there were 15 local organizations represented, and applications from eight others were presented for admission to the State group.

The Caddo-Bossier Association was chartered June 26, 1954. Almost from the date of its conception, members of the Association rallied behind Morley Hudson, well known in Shreveport as a successful businessman, as the natural leader of the group. At first a member of the board of directors, he later served as executive director of the Association. All his work has been done on a voluntary basis and without thought of remuneration.

From the start, Hudson leaned heavily upon his fellow Rotarians for assistance in obtaining a place in the sun for mentally retarded children. Harry A. Johnson, Jr., an attorney, prepared the charter for the State organization and set up its constitution and by-laws. He and another Rotarian, the Reverend John J. Rasmussen, a clergyman, served on the initial board of directors.

Publicity for the Underserved

Doug Attaway, Jr., and George Shannon, managing editor and editor, respectively, threw the weight of the Shreveport *Journal* behind the movement, and stories about mentally retarded children began appearing for the first time in the daily newspaper. Fellow Rotarian Charles A. Hazen, managing editor of Shreveport's other daily, the *Times*, also lent support to the Association through its columns.

Rotarians Tom McElroy, E. Newton Wray, and T. B. Langford lent the facilities of their motion-picture, television, and radio firms, respectively, in support of the movement. Residents of Caddo and Bossier Parishes, long accustomed to a hush-hush attitude toward those who were "not quite right," began receiving matter-of-fact information on the subject of mental retardation from all news-disseminating mediums.

By September of that first year, Rotarian Hudson had prevailed upon the Caddo Parish School Board to open three special classes in the public schools for white mentally retarded children and two classes for Negro youngsters. Heretofore, there had been no facilities for the training and education of these children save in private homes, which few of the parents could afford.

Hudson appeared before civic, fraternal, church, and social groups at every opportunity to explain the aims of the Association and to plead for assistance. At times he made as many as eight or ten addresses a week on behalf of mentally retarded children. When his commitments became impossibly heavy, Dr. W. L. McLeod, also a clergyman member of the Shreveport Rotary Club, filled in for him on radio, television, and speaker's platform. Dr. McLeod also rallied the clergy behind the movement.

Developing Alternatives

Despite the special classes operating under the school board's jurisdiction, there still remained the problem of those mentally retarded children who either were not educable or who had to receive social training before qualifying for admission to the special classes. Rotarian Hudson decided a workshop for mentally retarded children was the answer to the needs of these youngsters, some 24 of them in Shreveport alone.

However, the organization, still in its infancy, had no funds for the establishment of such a workshop. Hudson, with characteristic directness, went to Jesuit priests of St. John's Catholic Church in Shreveport and placed the problem before them. They offered him the use of an old residence, owned by the church, for establishment of the workshop.

This house was converted into five classrooms and a handicraft shop, with parents of the youngsters doing much of the remodelling work themselves. Rotarians donated equipment and supplies and, where this was impossible, saw to it that the organization received the necessary articles at cost.

Meanwhile, the Most Reverend Charles P. Greco, bishop of the Catholic diocese of Alexandria, became interested in the movement through reports reaching him through the priests of St. John's parish. The bishop and Rotarian Hudson had several long and earnest conferences. Soon Bishop Greco announced plans for the conversion of a lovely old estate in Clarks, Louisiana, into St. Mary's Residential Training School under auspices of the Catholic prelates of the diocese. Lucy Hudson was among the first of the children to be entered in the training school, the first of its kind in Louisiana.

With Lucy happily established in a school near enough so that he could visit her frequently, her father turned again to the problem of financing operation of the workshop for retarded children in Shreveport. For advice he called upon Rotarian W. J. Clark, veteran of many a local fund-raising campaign. Clark advised on the timing and planning of the first campaign, which netted some $10,000 in 1954. These funds were used to engage three teachers and three aides for the workshop.

Rotarians, as individuals or as heads of business and industrial firms, contributed more than 50 percent of the funds in that initial drive. The Shreveport Rotary Club also is paying the expenses of one youngster at the workshop on a scholarship basis. One Rotarian, C. L. Perry, serves as an administrative counsellor, while another, W. R. Barrow, acts as liaison man between the Caddo-Bossier Association and the Community Council on such matters as fund raising, programs, and projected plans for the future.

Never-failing help and encouragement also have been forthcoming from H. C. Anderson. Past Director of Rotary International, and from E. Allen Gillispie, current District Governor and long-time Secretary of the Shreveport Club. Both have lent the official approval of the Shreveport Rotary Club to undertakings of the Caddo-Bossier Association and also assisted in the successful $15,000 fund-raising campaign of 1955, concluded in December.

While the local workshop thrives and provides socialization and habit training for mentally retarded children in the two-parish area around Shreveport, the residential training school at Clarks, in Caldwell Parish, also is flourishing with the help of Rotarians. Q. T. Hardtner, president of the famed Urania Lumber Company of Urania, just seven miles south of Clarks, hauls equipment and supplies to the school without charge.

A Program Spreads

Word of the spectacular success of the Caddo-Bossier Association for Mentally Retarded Children has been spreading rapidly, and Morley Hudson has been called upon to assist in the formation of local associations in Arkansas, Texas, Mississippi, and adjoining States. He spends virtually as much time on the road in behalf of mentally retarded children as he does behind the desk of his own office.

Through all the long months of his often-discouraging efforts (which were later softened a bit by the arrival a year ago of a third daughter, Courtney, who is perfectly normal), Rotarian Hudson has been fully aware of the fact that none of the special classes, none of the workshop facilities, can benefit his own little daughter. Lucy always will hover midway between life and death in the land of the living dead.

"I'd give my right eye just to hear her call me 'Daddy,'" he says. "Since there is virtually nothing I can do to help Lucy, the next best thing is to help other mentally retarded children. I used to ask myself why this had happened to me. I have the answer now."

Creating a National Plan to Assist People with Mental Disabilities

Stafford L. Warren

In 1961 President John F. Kennedy publicly acknowledged that the United States had been ignoring the problems of the mentally retarded and pledged to find solutions to their issues. As a first step, Kennedy convened the President's Panel on Mental Retardation and asked it to prepare a National Plan to Combat Mental Retardation. The committee returned with ninety-five broad recommendations that included the innovative step of moving individuals with mental retardation out of the institution and back into their home environment. These recommendations were among the first to officially recognize the rights of the disabled. Stafford L. Warren was the Special Assistant to the President for Mental Retardation from 1962–63.

In October 1961, the late President John F. Kennedy launched the attack against mental retardation with these words: "We as a nation have for too long postponed an intensive search for solutions to the problems of the mentally retarded. That failure should be corrected." He took the first steps toward correcting that failure just six days later when he appointed the President's Panel on Mental Retardation and asked them to prepare a National Plan to Combat Mental Retardation.

Expert Recommendations

In October 1962, one and a half months ahead of its deadline, the Panel submitted its recommendations to the President. Shortly thereafter, the Office of the Special Assistant to the

Stafford L. Warren, "Implementation of the President's Program on Mental Retardation," *American Journal of Psychiatry*, vol. 121, December 1964, pp. 549–554. Copyright © 1964 American Psychiatric Association. Reprinted with permission from *American Journal of Psychiatry*.

President was created on the premise that action on the Executive level could move the program ahead at the necessary pace. I was chosen for the post and asked to work with Federal, State and private groups to carry out the recommendations of the Panel for legislative action and to increase public awareness of the condition.

Some of the main recommendations of the Panel's Report are: 1. Research on the causes of mental retardation and research into methods of care, rehabilitation and learning. 2. Preventive health measures, including a strengthened program of maternal and infant care; protection against known hazards to pregnancy; and extended diagnostic and screening services. 3. Strengthened educational programs generally and extended and enriched programs of special education. 4. More comprehensive and improved clinical and social services. 5. Improved methods and facilities for care. 6. A new legal, as well as social, concept for the retarded. 7. Help to overcome serious problems of insufficient professional manpower in the research, educational, administrative and service areas. 8. Programs of education and information to increase public awareness of the problem of mental retardation.

In general the concept is to decentralize the care of the retardate and retain all of the normal influences upon him of his home and community. In its entirety, the Panel Report offers 95 broad recommendations. These recommendations are our blueprint for action; the program to combat mental retardation is geared to their implementation.

Funding for Programs

The 88th Congress passed two very important bills which President Kennedy had signed just before his death. These bills provide each State with funds for planning programs dealing with mental retardation. There are additional matching maternal health and child welfare prenatal-postnatal care funds to be used for the prevention of prematurity, infections, birth injuries and malnutrition—all related to a preventive program in women who have a high risk of bearing children with mental retardation or brain injury. There are matching construction funds for research institutes; teaching, diagnostic and treatment units; community diagnostic and treatment units; and mental health diagnostic and treatment units. There are unmatched funds for projects and programs in special education and the teaching of teachers for the retarded.

Of course, the construction bills for medical education facilities and the general education bills which have been passed this last session are supportive in a general way by increasing the numbers of badly needed specialists in the medical, health and educational fields. Just as was the case in the Mental Health programs of former years this is seed money—a starter to show the way. There is much more to do, both by the Congress and by the States and the communities.

The Next Step

The next step in implementation is to activate State and local and private participation in carrying out the planning and the identification of the designated agency. Then comes organizing, designing, building and operating the many new units which each community needs. It took a great nationwide and community effort to get these bills passed by Congress. They will serve no useful purpose unless the States and local groups proceed to carry out their programs—whether those programs be medical, health and welfare, education or rehabilitative. The needs are very great and growing. Professional leadership is needed in each community, as well as in each clinic.

A Complex Issue

Mental retardation is a complex field. But part of the fascination of the problem is its complexity. There is, for example, a large unsolved problem area focused around the family of the severely retarded baby. The sociological, religious, medical and legal aspects require coordinated efforts, and, in addition, a coordinator. Few doctors or clergymen are familiar with all the complexities of such a situation, and fewer still are willing to accept an active role of leadership.

The problem does not narrow down to a simple question of whether or not the child should be placed in an institution. There are numerous other questions to be considered: How severe is the retardation and what is the prognosis? Is there a physical as well as a mental handicap? Is mental illness present? How severe are these complications? What community facilities and services are available for day care, residential care, training, therapy, rehabilitation and consultation? What are the costs of the services? What is the financial state of the family? What is the home environment? What is the attitude of the parents? Does consideration of the child come first? Or the parents? Or the family unit? Or the neighborhood? Or all of them at once? What is the best choice to take leadership in helping the parents to find answers to these questions and many more? Is it the doctor, the clergy? All too often the parents have not been able to find a focal point from which acceptable counsel and guidance might come.

Thus in the main, the latter question remains unanswered. When it is everybody's business it often becomes nobody's business. Heretofore mental retardation has been more ignored or put aside rather than being *anybody's* business.

Focusing on the Mildly on Moderately Affected

Consider the role of the mildly or moderately retarded adolescent in society, his needs for a slower-paced education, for adaptation of his skills in the lower levels of the labor market, for counseling, for better orientation and follow-up in employment. How can his legal rights be better protected? Is he being trained to handle a paycheck as well as a job? Or raise a family? In what ways can we enhance community-based efforts to keep him as self-sufficient as possible?

We can no longer ignore the early school dropout or the excuse that we need a large labor force of uneducated muscle men. An informed estimate is that automation is eliminating over one million of unskilled jobs a year. There is a constantly decreasing need for unskilled labor. Yet with training, the mildly retarded need not be unskilled and *automated jobs have much to offer the higher level retardate*.

Our present system of dealing with the unemployed is inadequate, in light of the fact that about one-third are thought to be retarded to some degree. There is a large problem of identification, evaluation and follow-up.

A Broad Perspective

These are but a few of the directions for inquiry suggested by the President's Panel Report. The "broad range approach" to mental retardation calls on the services of a tremendous variety of disciplines—general practitioners, obstetricians, pediatricians, neurologists, psychologists, anthropologists, special educators, the clergy as well as psychiatrists. We also need sociologists, lawyers, nurses, therapists,teachers, researchers, and a great number of those in the health-related fields.

• Mental retardation is not just a health problem; it is an educational and social problem as well. It is also a financial problem, and one of our main goals is to make taxpayers out of the five million or so potential tax consumers among the moderately and mildly retarded capable of being trained or educated.

Because of its complexity, no one discipline takes precedence over another in the field of mental retardation. It is not the prerogative of any branch of science of medicine or education or rehabilitation to claim prior rights over mental retardation, if, indeed, anyone wants the right. The problem calls for cooperation, coordination and inter-disciplinary action or the program cannot succeed at all.

Moving Away from Institutions

Until a few years ago [the early 1960s], almost the only professionals in contact with the mentally retarded were those in State and private mental hospitals. There was custodial care. But as to prevention, treatment and amelioration, there was a strange silence from all of the professions; from psychiatrists, pediatricians, obstetricians, and from medicine in general. Then there began to be a movement to get the retarded out of the large State institutions. This was done for a variety of reasons—partly economic, and quite understandably so. For the most part these patients did not require psychiatric treatment but only nursing, supervised or custodial care and some training if possible. The space was needed for those who would benefit more from the psychiatric services available.

At the same time, there was increasing pressure on the part of families of the mentally retarded for some constructive, positive program in their behalf. Some educators joined in this fight, along with a few physicians, a handful of legislators, and then of course, the President himself. . . .

Learning from Past Practices

In general it may be said that we have many illustrations, projects, pilot programs, even old established institutions, where good practices yield good—even spectacular—results. What formerly were considered to be hopeless situations have shown amelioration. Environmental, cultural and educational influences offer the great hope for all but particularly in the case of the mildly retarded, which make up by far the greatest number. . . .

We are just beginning to learn the interrelatedness of many aspects of life. Consequently questions constantly arise which require teamwork to find the answers. No one man nor any one discipline can find the answers yet to these and all the other questions we are now asking about this life we live. The answers are going to come only when we work together as we have done in the past, to find them.

Increased Access for the Disabled Is Mandated by Law

U.S. Department of Justice, Civil Rights Division

Advocacy by parents, friends, and support groups of the disabled resulted in federal legislation called the Americans with Disabilities Act (ADA) passed in 1990 that prohibits discrimination on the basis of disability and requires that "reasonable accommodation" be made in public places, including the workplace, for those with physical or mental disabilities. In the following selection, the U.S. Department of Justice, Civil Rights Division—the department responsible for enforcing the ADA—reports on the progress of the ADA seventeen years after it was signed into law.

Americans with disabilities face very real hurdles to enjoying the same educational, economic, and social opportunities as other Americans with no disabilities. Consider the following Census Bureau statistics drawn from the 2002 Survey of Income and Program Participation, some of the most recent government figures available.

Americans with disabilities, on average, continue to attain a lower level of education than those without disabilities. For example, almost 27 percent of adults ages 25 to 64 with a severe disability did not graduate from high school. By comparison, 14.6 percent of individuals with a non-severe disability and 10.4 percent of individuals with no disability failed to graduate from high school. Out of people ages 25–64, 43.1 percent of those without a disability graduated from college, compared with 32.5 percent of individuals with a non-severe disability and just 21.9 percent of those with a severe disability.

U.S. Department of Justice, Civil Rights Division, "Access for All: Five Years of Progress. A Report from the Department of Justice on Enforcement of the Americans with Disabilities Act," 2007.

In addition, American adults with disabilities, on average, are poorer and are far more likely to be unemployed than those adults without disabilities. For example, median earnings for people with no reported disability were $25,000, compared with $22,000 for people with a non-severe disability and $12,800 for those with a severe disability. In addition, more than one-fourth (25.7 percent) of individuals with no disability had household incomes of $80,000 or more, in comparison with 18.1 percent of people with a non-severe disability and 9.2 percent of individuals with a severe disability. Approximately 56 percent of adults ages 21–64 who had a disability were employed at some point in the one-year period prior to participating in the survey. People with severe disability status reported the lowest employment rate (42 percent), compared with the employment rates of people with non-severe disabilities (82 percent) and those with no disability (88 percent). Almost 27 percent of adults ages 25–64 with a severe disability live in poverty. By contrast, 11.2 percent of individuals with a non-severe disability and 7.7 percent of individuals with no disability live in poverty. Out of adults 65 years of age and older, 15 percent with a severe disability live in poverty, while 8.2 percent of individuals with a non-severe disability and 5.9 percent of individuals with no disability live in poverty. Finally, many Americans with disabilities live outside the economic and social mainstream of American life. Adults with disabilities have a lower likelihood of living with family than adults without disabilities. People with disabilities were more likely than people without disabilities to live alone or with non-relatives: among people 25 to 64 years old, 18.9 percent without disabilities lived alone or with non-relatives, compared with 23 percent with a non-severe disability and 27.8 percent with a severe disability. People 25 to 64 years old with a severe or non-severe disability were more likely to be the householder in a male- or female-headed household (12.7 percent) than people without a disability (8.8 percent). Of those ages 15 to 64, 36 percent with a severe disability used a computer, and 29 percent used the Internet at home. By contrast, individuals with a non-severe disability or with no disability had substantially better computer access with 60.7 percent using a computer and 50.9 percent using the Internet at home.

Daily Hurdles

In addition to these figures, the data from a 2004 Survey conducted by the National Organization on Disability in conjunction with the Harris polling organization provides further insight into hurdles faced by persons with disabilities in enjoying community opportunities. According to the survey, persons with disabilities are twice as likely as those without to have inadequate transportation (31 percent compared to 13 percent), have a higher likelihood of going without medical care (18 percent compared to 7 percent), and are less likely to socialize, eat out, or attend religious services. In addition, a full one-third of individuals with disabilities using assistive technology say they would lose their independence without it, illustrating its fundamental importance in promoting independent living.

These problems were entrenched due to a long history of shameful hostility to and fear of people with disabilities. Such hostility and fear produced outright discrimination and exclusion, and in some cases, forced sterilization and unnecessary institutionalization. Moreover, even some well-intentioned social policies had the effect of promoting dependency and isolation rather than independence and involvement in the community. . . .

The Goals of the ADA

The Americans with Disabilities Act (ADA), is a comprehensive civil rights law that provides a national mandate for the elimination of discrimination on the basis of disability in employment, state and local government programs and services, public accommodations, commercial facilities, transportation, and telecommunications. . . . The Civil Rights Division of the Department of Justice is deeply engaged in this battle on all of these fronts.

The goal of the ADA is simple—to open up all aspects of American life to people with disabilities. For too long, people with disabilities were held back by old modes of thinking and old methods of building. Prevailing attitudes made it hard for people with disabilities to get an education or to get a job. Barriers in society prevented people with disabilities from getting where they needed to go to build a better life.

The Sections of ADA

The ADA prohibits discrimination on the basis of disability in employment, state and local government activities, public accommodations, commercial facilities, transportation, and telecommunications. The Department of Justice enforces the provisions that apply to more than seven million places of public accommodation, including all hotels, restaurants, retail stores, theaters, health care facilities, convention centers, parks, and places of recreation (Title III), in all activities of state and local governments (Title II), and in all employment practices of state and local government employers with 15 or more employees (Title I).

The ADA also establishes architectural accessibility requirements for new construction and alterations of buildings and facilities covered under Title II and Title III, which generally include all nonresidential buildings and facilities.

ADA Enforcement

ADA enforcement and technical assistance activities cover more than seven million businesses and nonprofit agencies, more than 80,000 units of state and local government, and more than 100 federal agencies and commissions in the Executive Branch, touching over 50 million people with disabilities as well as their families and friends.

The Civil Rights Division has pioneered a multitrack approach to protecting the rights of individuals with disabilities—promoting expanded opportunities through cooperative compliance assistance, providing technical assistance, and backing these efforts with a robust enforcement program. Since the beginning of the New Freedom Initiative, the Department of Justice has secured positive results for people with disabilities in over 2000 actions including lawsuits, settlement agreements, and successful mediations.

The success of this multitrack approach is evident. Attitudes are changing and barriers are coming down all across America. The message of the ADA is being heard far and wide because the message of the ADA is freedom—freedom to contribute to society and freedom to enjoy the incredible opportunities our country provides.

The Effects of the ADA

The ADA is bringing about significant changes in our home-towns and communities. Thanks to the ADA, people with disabilities are participating in unprecedented numbers in civic life and are gaining equal access to the benefits and services that local government provides. All across America, towns and communities are taking steps to make their programs and services accessible. Town halls and courthouses across America are installing ramps and providing accessible parking and restrooms. The use of sign language interpreters and assistive listening devices is increasing at public meetings and in court proceedings, allowing full participation by people who are deaf or hard of hearing. Our police are improving communication with deaf citizens in the arrest process, and public safety officials are saving lives by making 9-1-1 systems directly accessible to those who use TTY's (teletypewriters) to communicate over the phone system. Communities are reshaping recreation and social service programs to allow full access by people with disabilities.

The ADA facilitates access by people with disabilities to all aspects of the free market system. The ADA's reach extends to recreational activities, shopping, business and leisure travel, and health care. Travel opportunities have expanded. Rental car companies increasingly provide cars with hand controls, and hotels across the country provide a widening array of accessible hotel rooms. Other barriers to transportation across the country have fallen as well. Most public buses now have lifts, and private transit—from airport shuttle vans to over-the-road buses—are becoming accessible in increasing numbers. Medical care is more accessible due to the proliferation of sign-language interpreter services, accessible rooms, and accessible examination tables.

New Technology Transforms the Lives of Disabled Individuals

Adam Schwartz

Adaptive computer technology has transformed the lives of many disabled individuals, argues Adam Schwartz in the following viewpoint. Through use of specially designed devices such as braille keyboards, says the author, many more individuals can achieve academic success and perform jobs previously unaccessible to them. Adam Schwartz has contributed pieces to Talking History, the Voice of America, and the BBC.

The computer revolution has made life easier for many. But for people with disabilities, computers are more than just a convenience—they're something of a miracle. A growing number of universities are providing "adaptive" or "assistive" technology to help their disabled students and staff with their studies and their careers. Adam Schwartz takes us to the Adaptive Technology Center (ATC) on the campus of Indiana University in Bloomington, Indiana.

Tucked into a quiet corner on the first floor of Indiana University Main Library, a young man sits at a computer terminal. He's typing, but looking away from the computer screen, which is as dark as his sunglasses. Next to him, a young woman is hunched over her keyboard, a metal cane at her feet. She's not looking at her screen either, which displays rows of Braille lettering as black dots on a white background. Both are blind. At Indiana University's Adaptive Technology Center, disabilities such as blindness, low vision and limited mobility don't matter as much as they do in the outside world. Here, they are overcome through computer technology.

Adam Schwartz, "Adaptive Technology Helps Disabled Students Succeed," VOANews .com, May 19, 2003.

"Through adaptive technology we're able to change lives, one life at a time, through one accommodation at a time," said Margaret Londergan, who created the ATC in 1999 after realizing that many students with disabilities were not aware of the new hardware and software that was available for them. She envisioned a resource center at the University that would give students access to the tools they needed to achieve academic success.

"I chose to go into this line of work because I believe in the potential of every individual, and by providing adaptive technology, we maximize the opportunity for individuals to reach their potential," she said.

Adaptive technology refers to computer hardware and software that has been developed specially for use by people with disabilities. The Center has a variety of software applications with odd names like Jaws, Zoomtext, and Dragon Naturally Speaking. It also has some unusual hardware, like a keyboard that requires just the slightest touch of the fingertips, and a computer mouse that's operated with a foot rather than a hand. Since the Center opened, 2,000 students have taken advantage of high-tech tools like these.

Delia Thompson works inside a soundproof booth at the Adaptive Technology Center. She's printing out a textbook in Braille for a blind student from Korea who's in an intensive English program. The printer turns out a sheet of stiff, white paper embossed with rows of raised dots.

Printed materials for the blind have been available since the mid-1800s, when Louis Braille developed an alphabet of raised dots that could be read with the fingertips. But creating pages of Braille text has always been a laborious process, and as a result, books in Braille have been few and expensive. But with computer technology, that's all changed. Now any manuscript can be quickly and inexpensively turned into a Braille book.

Ms. Thompson, who has been blind since birth, works here full-time, converting written text into Braille books. She says she prefers to do things for herself rather than rely on others.

"I'm a very strong advocate for independence," she said.

Computers have made that self-sufficiency possible. Once, when a blind person wanted to get some reading done, he or she would have had to depend on a sighted assistant to read out loud. But now, using adaptive technology, Ms. Thompson can read on her own.

"I wouldn't have gone through college if adaptive technology didn't exist," she said. "[If it weren't for] computers, then I think blind people would be totally lost."

She can answer her e-mail, use the Internet, and create documents with a word processing program. She reads the text on a device called a Braille display, which is roughly the size and shape of an ordinary computer keyboard. But instead of keys, a row of hundreds of little metal pins runs across the length of the display. The pins pop up to form Braille letters, which Ms. Thompson reads like she would Braille dots printed on paper, with her fingertips, moving swiftly from left to right. When she reaches the end of a line, she presses a button on the display. The pins drop and then immediately pop up again in a new arrangement, with the next line of text.

Moira Roberts, 29, is a graduate student in Indiana University's [IU] School for Public and Environmental Affairs, and one of the IU students who use the Adaptive Technology Center. She has dyslexia, a learning disorder that makes it very hard for her to read.

"I have problems comprehending what I'm reading. I read extremely slowly," she said. "I can read, it's not that I can't. But not on a graduate level. I read at an eighth grade level."

Ms. Roberts was accustomed to getting top grades in undergraduate school. But when she entered the master's program, she could no longer get around her dyslexia.

"When you get to the graduate level, you're doing so much reading, it was just too much for me, and although those little tricks of the trade that you always use to get yourself over, no longer work, when you get to a certain level," she said.

Dyslexia made graduate school so hard for her that she considered dropping out. That's when she learned about the Adaptive Technology Center and a screen-reading program called Kurzweil 3000. The Kurzweil allows her to read faster with better comprehension.

It all begins with a razor blade. The first step in preparing a book to be read in the Kurzweil 3000 is to cut Ms. Roberts' textbook apart. The pages must be removed so they can be fed into a scanning machine.

Technician Tomas Gregg feeds the loose pages into the high-speed machine, which converts the written words into digitized text. Then, the text is recorded onto a compact disc.

"Let's see. Here's your books, and here's your CD of your books digitized," he said.

At her computer, Moira Roberts puts the CD into the drive. The text of her book appears on her monitor and a synthesized voice begins to read.

On screen, the text is highlighted in color. The current sentence is in yellow and the word that's being read is in bright green. This way, Ms. Roberts can see and hear the words at the same time, making it easier for her to understand what she's reading. The software allows her to set the reading speed and choose from different synthesized voices.

Ms. Roberts no longer thinks about dropping out of graduate school. With the help of the Kurzweil, she's nearly completed her master's program. Since the Adaptive Technology Center opened, it has become a model for similar enterprises around the United States. In the years ahead, adaptive technology is expected to become even more sophisticated, giving people with disabilities even more opportunities to follow their dreams.

CHAPTER 2

Current Issues Faced by People with Disabilities

Chapter Preface

In the 2002 analysis of recent census data, 51.2 million people (18.1 percent of the U.S. population) reported some level of disability and 32.5 million (11.5 percent of Americans) reported having a severe disability. The census data also confirmed that individuals with disabilities are found in all racial, ethnic, and socioeconomic groups. Given the large number of disabled people in the United States, it is expected that concerns such as quality of life, education, and rights for individuals would be vigorously debated among lawmakers, national organizations, parents, family members, and individuals with disabilities. However, despite the large number of disabled Americans now and throughout history, the current climate of open dialog regarding people with disabilities did not come about until the early 1960s.

At that time debates regarding institutionalization, independent living, and education were thrust into the public spotlight as advocates fought to raise their disabled children in the community rather than in institutions and as disabled adults fought for the right to live independently. Over the following decade, the disability rights movement became more organized and developed a specific mission: to improve the quality of life of people with disabilities. Specifically, to increase areas of access and safety for people with physical disabilities and to increase acceptance of mentally challenged persons in the workforce and the community.

The first challenge for disabled people and their advocates was to attack the long-held belief that segregation benefited both the disabled and general society. In order to focus attention on the the bias against the disabled and ultimately to change misconceptions about them, activists staged demonstrations, attracted media attention, and organized fundraising drives. Together with disability rights pioneers such as

Ed Roberts, who fought for disabled access at the University of California, Berkeley, and groups such as the National Association for Retarded Children (now called The ARC), over a thirty-year period the disabled met their objectives of deinstitutionalization, an increased community presence, and independent living conditions. In 1990 another hard-won victory occurred when President George H.W. Bush signed the Americans with Disabilities Act (ADA), a federal law guaranteeing civil rights protections to individuals with disabilities. Despite the gains made for equal rights and legislative protections, the disability rights movement continues to fight for individualized care, appropriate education, and increased access to public spaces.

Debates in the twenty-first century include concerns that the rush of deinstitutionalization has led to decentralized community services and group homes that lack oversight and quality of care, continued feelings that disabled people still face discrimination in employment, and social issues related to capital punishment for the mentally retarded. The viewpoints in this chapter focus on these specific controversies facing the disabled.

Dissolution of Institutions for the Disabled May Lead to Unsafe and Substandard Care

Meg LaPorte

Following the outcry over substandard institutions for individuals with mental retardation and developmental disabilities in the 1960s, many large institutions were shut down. In the following selection Meg LaPorte, of the American Medical Directors Association, discusses concerns that have arisen as many individuals affected by mental retardation and developmental disabilities are moved from institutions into community settings. LaPorte notes that the rush to deinstitutionalize the nation's disabled resulted in decentralized community services and group homes that lack oversight and quality of care.

In the Washington, D.C., suburb of Fairfax, Va., an expansive 86-acre campus of 12 buildings and nearly 500 employees is home to more than 180 men and women with mental retardation and development disabilities (MR/DD). As a state-run intermediate care facility for individuals with MR/DD (ICF/MR), and one of five such facilities run by the state, the Northern Virginia Training Center (NVTC) has become an anomaly among MR/DD service providers nationwide.

Since the inception of home- and community-based service (HCBS) waivers in 1981 and the subsequent furor of deinstitutionalization following the Supreme Court's *Olmstead [v. L.C. and E.W.]* decision in 1999, the landscape of MR/DD services has changed significantly. Facilities that historically served several hundred individuals in state-run centers have dramatically downsized to congregate housing settings serving six or fewer people.

Meg LaPorte, "Large ICFs/MR Being Phased Out: The Move Toward Community Settings Has Given Rise to Concerns About Quality and Safety," *Provider*, April 2006, pp. 20–30. Reproduced by permission.

Between 1960 and 2004, 174 state-run institutions, or special units of 16 or more persons with MR/DD, have closed in the United States. Some states have taken steps to close all of their state-run institutions in favor of building smaller group homes or transferring funds to less expensive community programs. In 1991, New Hampshire became the first state to close all of its public institutions. Since then, the District of Columbia, Alaska, Hawaii, Maine, New Mexico, Rhode Island, Vermont, and West Virginia have followed suit, and nine more large facilities serving individuals with MR/DD are slated for closure before the end of 2007. Only 12 states remain in which at least one state-operated institution has not been closed.

There Is Still a Need for Institutions

"There needs to be a continuum of benefits for individuals with MR/DD," says Marilyn Weber, superintendent of Weber Health Care Center in Wellington, Ohio. "There is a place for waivers in our system, but residents of ICFs/MR are reflective of the normal population: They are not homogenous. Many have chronic medical needs."

Weber, who is chair of the American Health Care Association's MR/DD committee, notes that there is an obvious good side of HCBS expansion: affordability of choice and options, including the ability to choose not to live in a state-operated facility. On the negative side, there has been a reduction in funding and, in some states like Ohio, a push to remove the entitlement program for ICFs/MR, she says.

A New Look

For 37 consecutive years, the number of individuals with MR/DD served by large state-run facilities has declined steadily, by an average 4 percent each year. More recently, from 2002 to 2004, the population residing in these facilities dropped by 7 percent, from 44,451 to 41,214. And all states, except Colorado and North Dakota, have reduced their public institutional populations during the period between 2002 to 2004.

Of the 148,520 total residential (public and private) MR/DD settings in 2004, 147,460 had 15 or fewer residents, and 140,584 had six or fewer residents. The estimated 145,136 non-state settings with 15 or fewer residents made up 98.4 percent of all settings of this type.

According to the "National Health Interview Survey on Disability and the Residential Information Systems Project," an estimated 92 percent of all Americans with MR/DD live with family members, spouses, or alone; 6 percent live in community-supported living arrangements; 1 percent live in large institutions; and another 1 percent reside in nursing facilities.

While larger facilities are rapidly disappearing, there has been a steady increase in the total number of people with MR/DD receiving residential services. Between 1977 and 2004, for example, the total number of residential service recipients grew by 58.9 percent, from 247,780 to an estimated 420,202. Total population increases in that 26-year span, both state and non-state, were limited to placements in settings with 15 or fewer residents.

Closure Versus Choice

The radical move toward downsizing of facilities over the past 30 years has left an aging stock of larger institutions—where such institutions exist at all. Virginia's NVTC, for example, was built in 1973, and its architecture is reminiscent of that period's industrial-style flat roofs and gray concrete exteriors. But a closer look reveals a more vital facility flanked by nature trails, a pavilion, and gardens that are kept up by the residents and maintenance staff. Inside this self-contained community is a tightly knit network of staff, parents, and volunteers who serve a range of clients, from individuals who are extremely low-functioning with diagnoses of moderate or profound mental retardation—some with extreme maladaptive behaviors—to higher-functioning individuals who work in the campus' skills training center recycling soft drink containers and boxes or posting mass mailings for local organizations.

Alice Mary Hymel, a staff social worker, views NVTC as an integral part of the surrounding suburban community, and she's adamant about the facility's importance in the spectrum of care for individuals with MR/DD.

"There is a place for HCBS, but there also is a need for facilities like NVTC," she says. "We are also very tied to the community."

But others in the state see the facility and others like it as remnants of a bygone age. Virginia's legislature is in the process of approving a controversial plan that would restructure the state's MR/DD services, following former Gov. Mark Warner's (D) proposal in late 2005 to close one of the five state facilities and restructure two others. The proposal, known as Virginia's System Transformation Initiative, has drawn the ire of many MR/DD advocacy groups and landed parents and caregivers on both sides of an issue that spans years of cultural and medical practices.

Unlike many other states that have committed to phasing out their large facilities, Virginia's plan combines downsizing of the state-run facilities with plans to bolster MR/DD services to clients living in the community.

"The training centers are in immediate need of physical improvements," says Lee Price, Virginia director of mental retardation services. "We want to do what's right for all of our clients—in the community and in facilities." Price notes that the infrastructure and services need to be in place before the state department begins moving hundreds of people into the community.

Self-Determination

Historically, children with a diagnosis of moderate to severe mental retardation were automatically placed in institutions. But according to MR/DD advocates, society has evolved, and the culture of caring for children with MR/DD has changed. Proponents of a movement known as self-determination believe that most, if not all, individuals with mental retardation can be cared for at home or in a more integrated community setting.

"Today, younger parents of individuals with MR/DD are adamantly opposed to putting their children in a facility," says Nancy Mercer, executive director of The Arc of Northern Virginia.

The Virginia initiative, for example, includes plans to rebuild two of the training centers to create "smaller, more efficient state-of-the-art" facilities, in addition to boosting the MR/DD waiver rates by 10 percent for congregate living services and 5 percent for all other waiver services.

But downsizing one center to a 300-bed facility and the other to a 100-bed facility was not the "state of the art" that Mercer had in mind. She contends that Virginia has a unique opportunity to finally make a dramatic shift from large state-run facilities to community care. "I don't think it's necessary to have large institutions for people with mental retardation," Mercer says. "The stigma of integrating these individuals has diminished, and there are now many resources within the community."

Jane Anthony begs to differ. Her son Jason has been living at NVTC for 28 years, and she strongly believes that large facilities like NVTC must remain a vital part of the state's care system. "I cannot care for my son at home," she says. "He is best cared for at the training center where his activities are monitored around the clock."

Anthony notes that Jason has Pica, a condition that is common in people with developmental disabilities and can sometimes surface in children who've had a brain injury. People with Pica frequently crave and consume nonfood items such as dirt, cigarette butts, hair, soap, and even feces. Pica is considered to be a serious eating disorder that can sometimes result in severe health problems.

"I am thankful that my son is at NVTC," Anthony says. "With a functional level of a six- to eight-month-old, he has no comprehension of risks or consequences that come with living in a house," she says. "NVTC is truly home for him, and it's the least restrictive environment in which he can be safe and well cared for."

In response to Virginia's initiative, however, The Arc has proposed that any funds for replacing or restructuring state institutions should be spent only to address the immediate, life-threatening health and safety of current residents and that the state should reinvest in community living options for current facility residents and their families.

"Families should be able to choose from individualized community supports, sponsored placements, MR/DD waiver in-home services, small MR/DD waiver group homes, or four- to six-bed community" ICFs/MR, according to The Arc's proposal.

Mercer believes that, unless Virginia invests in community services appropriately, there will be a huge mushrooming of aging parents whose children will not have access to adequate services once they graduate from school, as children in public school systems get lots of services while community services are scarce. She also believes that, ultimately, given a perfect world, all parents would want their children at home.

Community Outreach

In the absence of a perfect world. Virginia plans to replicate in all its centers NVTC's outpatient Regional Community Services Center (RCSC). Started in 1996, the RCSC provides specialized medical, behavioral, dental, and respite services to individuals living in the community who have complex medical and behavioral needs.

Virginia's Department of Mental Retardation, Mental Health, and Substance Abuse Services considers RCSCs to be a key player in the transition of clients to the community as the centers downsize.

The fundamental goal is to ease the transition from living in a state-run facility to a community-based group home, according to the Virginia department.

Since Medicaid does not cover dental services for clients with MR/DD, the RCSC's dentists are constantly busy providing services to the NVTC clients, in addition to nearly 400 clients in the community.

"In Virginia, there are services available to people in institutions that are not available to people in the community," says Price. "The RCSCs will help bridge this gap."

Retaining Options

Tamie Hopp believes the haste to deinstitutionalize the nation's elderly and individuals with disabilities was sparked by a misinterpretation of what the 1999 Supreme Court's *Olmstead* decision required. "There were three parts to the *Olmstead* decision," says Hopp, who is executive director of VOR [Voice of the Retarded], a national MR/DD advocacy organization whose members include families. MR/DD organizations, and professionals. "Within the dicta of the Supreme Court's *Olmstead* decision is further clarification that while community living is a goal for most people, it cannot be imposed on someone. It has caused a misguided focus of some advocacy groups to get people out of institutions and fueled deinstitutionalization in the wrong direction."

Hopp claims that services at the community level are not as ideal as most would believe. "There are many cases of abuse and neglect in the community settings. And there have been state audits and media investigations in many states," she says.

While Hopp realizes that VOR is a lonely voice in the MR/DD community in respecting the value of ICFs/MR for individuals with complex needs, VOR continues to advocate for a "full range of quality residential options and services," including the home, community residences, and congregate and large facilities. VOR opposes efforts that eliminate options for persons with mental retardation, medically fragile conditions, and challenging behaviors and contends that the final determination of what is appropriate depends on the unique abilities and needs of the individual and desires of the family and guardians.

Unlike VOR, the Alliance for Full Participation in America, a national coalition of organizations serving the DD field, seeks to end the institutionalization of all people with MR/DD. Among the alliance's members are the American Association on Mental Retardation (AAMR), the Arc of the United States, the National Association of Councils on Developmental Disabilities, and the National Association of Directors of Developmentally Disabled Services (NADDDS).

"Full participation and integration into the community, is akin to a civil rights issue for many advocates," Mercer says.

But nearly 80 percent of the individuals residing in large ICFs/MR have severe and profound mental retardation and require around-the-clock care for their own safety, VOR says.

According to VOR, almost half of these residents have two or more additional conditions, and nearly all need help walking, toileting, eating, dressing, and communicating verbally. In contrast, the vast majority of MR/DD individuals who reside in the community have higher functioning levels and need little or no intensive care services, VOR says.

Meanwhile, the attitudes expressed by the alliance are winning out. The rapid growth of HCBS waivers and fallout from the *Olmstead* decision have given momentum to a phenomenon known as self-determination. The basic concept is that beneficiaries should be able to direct their Medicaid dollars toward the services of their choice, be it adult day care or personal assistance.

In 1997, the Robert Wood Johnson Foundation established the Self-Determination Program for Persons with Developmental Disabilities. The foundation granted a total of $5 million to 19 states to "explore consumer-directed alternatives to providing long-term care services to individuals with a developmental disability."

This set the stage for organizations like The Arc of the United States and AAMR [now known as AIDD], a national MR/DD advocacy organization, to focus on promoting the movement. According to these groups, individuals must have opportunities and experiences that enable them to exert control in their lives and to advocate on their own behalf. In a December 2004 position statement, the two organizations asserted that, "as self advocates, people with MR/DD have the same right to self-determination as all people and must have the freedom, authority, and support to exercise control over their lives."

The statement outlined a list of rights that individuals with MR/DD must have, including the opportunity to advocate for themselves with the knowledge that their desires will be heard and respected; the opportunity to vote and to become active members and leaders on community boards, committees, and agencies; and the ability to hire, train, manage, and fire their personal assistants.

The position statement further called on other disability organizations to make self-determination a priority and include this important concept in their publications, advocacy, training, policies and research.

"Many of our constituents have not had the opportunity or the support to control choices and decisions about important aspects of their lives. Instead, they are often overprotected and involuntarily segregated," the statement says. "Many of these people have not had opportunities to learn the skills and have the experiences that would enable them to take more personal control and make choices, and the lack of such learning opportunities and experiences have impeded their right to become participating, valued, and respected members of their communities.". . .

Unfortunate Consequences

According to The Arc of the United States, more than 90 percent of people with developmental disabilities will experience sexual abuse at some point in their lives, and 49 percent will experience 10 or more abusive incidents.

Other studies suggest that 39 to 68 percent of girls and 16 to 30 percent of boys will be sexually abused before their 18th birthday. Even more alarming is a 1994 study that found that 15,000 to 19,000 people with DD are raped each year in the United States.

It comes as no surprise then that the downside of states' efforts to reduce spending and increase community services increases the likelihood of abuse and neglect. Some advocates believe that the creation of waiting lists for HCBS waiver programs is one contributor to this increased risk.

Another consequence of HCBS growth is litigation on behalf of clients and their families, and some argue, a lack of quality assurance programs to ensure the appropriate and effective delivery of services that have shifted from previously state-run and -monitored institutions to community group homes.

A policy brief published by the University of Minnesota Research and Training Center on Community Living claims that people with significant and complex medical needs are a small percentage of people with MR/DD. Data about their health outcomes are also very limited, the center says.

Other research suggests that most people's health improves with a move to the community, while some data show that health outcomes for people with the most severe disabilities are slightly worse.

VOR says that since 1990, more than 47,000 people have been transferred from large, congregate residential facilities, while the number of persons living in smaller, community-based living arrangements more than doubled, from about 98,000 in 1990 to almost 239,000 in 2000. About half of these people (119,500) received residential services and supports in living arrangements for three or fewer people.

With the increased development of very small living arrangements, VOR fears that the concomitant increase in sites will become diffused throughout communities, thereby posing greater quality management and system infrastructure challenges for states and local developmental disabilities authorities.

With that in mind, VOR proposes that it is time that states step back, carefully consider the existing quality of their community service systems, and assess how those people now in the system are being served and how much money is needed to improve the system for current and future users.

The Autism Research Institute reported nearly 10 years ago that a study of 18,000 individuals with MR/DD in California from 1980 to 1992 found the death rate to be 72 percent higher in group homes than in large facilities.

Another study of 1,900 California clients that had transferred to group homes from facilities in 1993–1994 showed an 82 percent higher death rate in group homes. According to the report, both studies carefully matched all known risk factors for both institutional and community clients.

In 2004, 34 states reported having waiting lists for waiver services while 10 states said they had none. A Kaiser Foundation report revealed that since 2002, the number of waiver with waiting lists has grown to 102, with almost 207,000 individuals on waiting lists in 2004. Forty-five percent of those waiting for services are individuals with MR/DD.

The average length of time an individual spends on waiting lists varies by type of population, with MR/DD waivers holding the highest average at 25 months.

In 2003, the Government Accountability Office recommended that CMS [Centers for Medicaid and Medicare Services] take steps to better ensure that state quality assurance efforts are adequate to protect the health and welfare of HCBS waiver beneficiaries and to strengthen federal oversight of the growing HCBS waiver programs.

In response, CMS has bolstered its efforts to improve quality assurance among waiver programs through a renewed review of state waiver programs, making direct technical assistance available to states to strengthen their quality assurance/improvement systems, Promising Practices to spotlight innovative state HCBS, earmarking Real Choice grant dollars to assist states in quality assurance/improvement, and distributing quality tools for states.

In addition to continued growth of the self-determination movement, experts speculate that demographics and technological advances will play large roles in the future of MR/DD policies and program trends. Mercer concedes that many parents of children living in institutions have concerns about the lack of oversight and the quality of care in community services.

"I understand this concern because the state has not invested appropriately in community services," she says.

The Disabled Should Not Have to Live in Institutions

Karl Grunewald

In the following selection, Karl Grunewald, who served as a medical counselor at the National Board of Social Welfare in Sweden, strongly asserts his belief that no disabled individual should live in an institution. Grunewald notes that institutions were originally founded in a time of prejudice against individuals with disabilities. During this time, disabled individuals were sterilized against their will and isolated from society. The institutions were specifically founded to confine and restrict disabled individuals' access to the community. Grunewald feels that people with disabilities are psychologically damaged by living in institutions and should be allowed to live in other community settings.

In the 1920s the philanthropic approach to care for people with disabilities subsided as ideas concerning racial hygiene changed the way in which people with disabilities were viewed. The institutional system was developed and people with intellectual disabilities were increasingly isolated from society.

Trampled Rights in the Past

Forced sterilizations were performed in large numbers throughout the western part of the world, and in Germany, under the Nazi regime, a large number of intellectually disabled children, teenagers and adults were murdered.

No other group of people has been subject to the same levels of encroachment on their integrity, as well as prejudiced abuse as children and adults with intellectual disabilities. Despite the fact that the human rights include people with dis-

Karl Grunewald, *Close the Institutions for the Intellectually Disabled—Everyone Can Live in the Open Society: A Pamphlet on the European Year of People with Disabilities*, 2003, pp. 2–11. www.independentliving.org.

abilities, it is still considered acceptable to deny them access to the open society and confine them in institutions.

Today, the institutions are the last remaining manifestation of past, collective ideologies, that gave society the right, and the power, to separate certain people from the rest of the community and limit their freedom, influence and life conditions.

There is evidence that no people with disabilities need to live in institutions, no matter how profound their disabilities are. And more importantly: To live in the open society leads to an increased degree of independence and personal development.

Abolition of Institutions

In Sweden and Norway all institutions for people with intellectual disabilities have been closed. As a result, destructive behavioural patterns have diminished or disappeared altogether to a degree that no one could have foreseen. Prejudices have been torn down, the solidarity with people with intellectual disabilities has been strengthened and the humanitarian forces in society have gained influence.

Inclusive living has had no negative effects or consequences. Furthermore, in the long run it is more economically sound, due to the good results.

As a result, the right to live like you and I do has become a political issue.

The Psychological Effects of Being Institutionalized

A vast amount of research has been done on the psychological effects of living in an institution. In general, the negative effects are less severe when the institution is modern and small scale. But even in small institutions there is a marked difference compared to inclusive living.

The trauma of being involuntarily separated from one's parents, friends, and familiar home environment creates a fundamental conviction of being unwanted and powerless, of being an object, rather than a unique individual.

The institutional environment in itself creates additional handicaps that will mark the person for the rest of his or her life. It is primarily the emotional and social development that is hampered.

Emotional maturity is not dependent on the degree of disability. A person may be relatively intelligent, but emotionally immature, while someone with severe intellectual disabilities may be relatively mature, emotionally. The fact that a person with profound intellectual disabilities has difficulties in expressing his or her feelings does not preclude a developed emotional life.

The development of a normal emotional life is hampered when one is confined to a paltry and single-sexed environment, and suffers from lack of personal life, lack of autonomy and lack of respect for one's personal integrity.

Emotional immaturity leads to a hampered and underdeveloped identity development and delayed sexual maturity. Furthermore, the development of language, as well as the intellectual development, is also hampered to a greater degree than was previously known.

Progressive Effects

Children and youth tend to develop ways of stimulating themselves, sometimes in self-destructive ways. Adults develop various psychiatric symptoms, aggressiveness and depression being the most common ones, although the symptoms may be different for people with intellectual disabilities than for non-disabled persons.

As a result of the research on the psychological effects of living in an institution, two terms have been coined: social deprivation and taught helplessness. Together, these terms reflect the results this research has led to.

Some institutions work better than others, but not even the best ones reach the same qualitative levels as adequately supported inclusive groups does. The reasons for this are that the groups who live together are small, they live in residential areas, the working conditions for the staff are better and the residents have more contact with their relatives.

The Normalisation Principle

The overreaching idea is that children, youth, and adults with disabilities should be given access to living conditions and everyday routines that are as similar as possible to those of ordinary citizens.

Parents should be given support so that their children and teenagers can remain in the home. Only under inordinate circumstances should they be given the opportunity to live in a foster home or a pupil home.

Adults should be offered support so that they can live in a way similar to other adults or in a group home.

This way, persons with disabilities will avoid having their personalities shaped by living in an institution. Being part of the surrounding community will lead to new relationships and experiences.

By living like other people one will develop a personal daily rhythm as regards getting up in the morning, eating at regular hours, having work hours, leisure time, and bed time. In addition, this will lead to a normal weekly routine with opportunities to participate in cultural or other activities in one's neighbourhood, depending on one's individual interests.

A normal living situation will ease the contact with one's parents, relatives and friends, due to both social and geographical reasons. Having one's own apartment as part of the group home will make it possible to have control over one's own social life.

Just as for ordinary citizens, all residents of the group home and the pupil home should partake in daily activities—children should attend school and adults should have jobs to go to.

Children, youth and adults should live separately. Within larger districts there may be grounds for having special residences for young adults, as well as for older persons.

Within the frames for age divisions there should not be any divisions based on sex or degree of disability. In reality, this means that a group home should not house more than one person who has profound physical disabilities and is dependent on special aids for hygiene, etc.

The only groups of people who should live together because they share additional handicaps, apart from their intellectual disabilities, are deaf people, because they need staff who master sign language, and persons with autism, due to special treatment programs.

In order for the individual to become socially integrated—that is, that he or she is given the opportunity to develop relationships and participate in the community—an inclusive living [arrangement] is a prerequisite. This demands support and guidance, as well as an awareness of the amount of time it will take to reach these goals.

The Situation for the Staff

The work structure of the staff at institutions is more task oriented and based on routines, than that of the staff at inclusive living facilities. This means that they are responsible for certain tasks, for example in the kitchen, the bathroom, as regards cleaning, etc. The staff is part of a hierarchical structure and seldom have the opportunity to develop and improve the support themselves.

The staff at inclusive homes feel greater responsibility for the living facility, they show more involvement, they like their work place and their work structure is focused on the individual. Each of them is responsible for one or more residents, concerning everything that involves these individuals in the home. Their input can be adapted to the needs of each individual.

The Principle of the Small Group

A group of people with disabilities that live together should be no larger than that they can develop personal, lasting relationships with each other and with the staff. Because their communicatory skills, as well as their ability to predict different reactions, are limited, the group must be kept small.

Number of possible relationships rises dramatically with an increased size of the group. For example, a group of four people may, besides the fact that each one can relate to one of the other members, two can relate to one of the two remaining persons or three [can] relate to the fourth. Altogether, this amounts to 25 alternatives. In a group of five there are 90 such alternatives theoretically. Research and experience show that the best size is a group consisting of approximately four persons.

A residence for a small group will blend in with the rest of the neighbourhood and the size of the staff will be kept down. In a small group conflicts, as well as routines, will be few and the participation in society will increase. Each individual will be given the support he or she needs.

The Americans with Disabilities Act Provides Access to the American Dream

Tony Coelho

In the following selection, Tony Coelho, one of the authors of the Americans with Disabilities Act (ADA), reflects on the impact of the ADA. Coelho discusses the rationale behind the establishment of the ADA and his personal experience with epilepsy, which helped him to recognize the stigma and discrimination people with disabilities face in society. He feels that the ADA resulted in many positive changes in the United States that have benefited the disabled and average Americans alike.

Mr. Chairman, thank you very much for having these hearings and having me today [September 13, 2006]. And I appreciate the opportunity to testify.

Since I left [office] in 1989, I do not lobby or anything else. I seldom come back here [to Capitol Hill]. But this hearing is very important to me. So I am appreciative of the invitation from Chairman [F. James] Sensenbrenner to participate as a Majority witness here today.

The Rationale Behind the Act

I introduced the Americans with Disabilities Act (ADA) in 1988, together with Senator Lowell Weicker, when I served in the House. And I introduced it with Lowell because I thought it was very important that this legislation be both bicameral and bipartisan.

And I think that one of the important things for us to remember is that a lot of us, when we were in the Congress, we

Tony Coelho, "Testimony of the Honorable Tony Coelho, Chair, The Epilepsy Foundation, and Former Representative in Congress from the Central Valley District of California," *Americans with Disabilities Act: Sixteen Years Later*, hearing before the subcommittee on the constitution of the committee on the Judiciary House of Representatives, 109th Congress, 2nd session, September 13, 2006.

made a lot of promises about the ADA. Through the passage of the ADA, we promised our fellow Americans who have disabilities that they had the right to share in our country's greatest strengths: our capacity for progress and advancement.

I believe that the prosperity and justice are not meant to be hoarded but they are meant to be shared, that when the American dream is available to ever-greater numbers of us, that it in itself is the wellspring of our national security and prosperity. For generations of Americans the right and ability to work at a trade or a profession was the key to individual realization of that dream and the national prosperity that followed.

Personal Experiences Illuminate Greater Needs

My personal experience with epilepsy shaped my recognition of the need for legislation to address the stigma and discrimination people with disabilities face. As I learned when my epilepsy was discovered and legalized bigotry left me unemployed and unemployable, work means much more than financial stability.

My passion for expanding job opportunities for Americans with disabilities is rooted in my very life experiences, in the pain and personal failure I felt when I was prevented from working and in the competence and ability to contribute I rediscovered when I was finally able to find work once again.

I have always been outspoken about my disability. I believe that if you want to change people's perceptions, particularly of hidden and stigmatized disabilities like epilepsy, you have to be outspoken about it. People have to see that any one of us could be affected by a disability, that people with disabilities are not somehow other than those without. It can happen to your husband, your wife, your daughter, your son, your father, your mother, your best friend or your next-door neighbor at any time.

I introduced the Americans with Disabilities Act because I knew firsthand how a person could be qualified to do a job but still be excluded from employment because of others' misunderstandings and fears. I knew then, as now, that people with disabilities may be discriminated against because their condition is a disability or because the employer thinks it is a disability, even if it is not, in fact, substantially disabling or sometimes just because someone has a past history of a disability.

Even though my disability, my epilepsy, did not interfere with my ability to work or participate in everyday activities, I was unfairly denied many opportunities simply because of [the] stigma associated with my health condition and the ignorance of others. Stigma and ignorance about epilepsy persist today and still result in the denial of equal opportunity for many.

An Inclusive Legislation

There is similar stigma and ignorance about a whole range of other disabilities, which may be controlled to a certain extent, such as mental illness and diabetes, which likewise may effectively rob many others of their part of the American dream.

As the author of the ADA, I absolutely intended the legislation to cover people with disabilities who took medication or used a corrective device to alleviate their condition but were nonetheless denied employment or fired from employment because of their disability. I absolutely intended it to cover people whose conditions did not actually interfere with daily living but who were treated by others as having a disability.

I believe that everyone in the Congress—some of you who are here today—who voted to pass the bill understood that it applied to people like me. I intended this bill to apply to the discrimination that I faced in my family, in my church and in the Government because of my epilepsy.

The Impact of the ADA

The ADA has now become a model for anti-disability discrimination legislation around the world as more and more countries adopt civil rights protections that promote the full integration of people with disabilities and the protection of their civil rights.

America and Congress, when it passed the ADA, proposed a true model to the rest of the world because of our goal and dedication to the full inclusion of all Americans into the mainstream of life. This includes our understanding of the belief that people who have disabilities are fully capable of working in competitive employment and being productive members of society.

Sometimes a reasonable accommodation, one that is not unduly burdensome, is needed. Often it isn't.

The support of the ADA was bipartisan, bicameral and complete. We all understood that if we do not integrate people with disabilities we not only cause them and ourselves to suffer, we also expend enormous resources to support people who actually want and are capable of supporting themselves. That is a far different attitude and goal than many other countries have. Rather, attitudes of paternalism, caretaking and exclusion are the norm.

Though we have a long way to go internationally, we continue to be a standard bearer in this area of the law for the rest of the world. You should be proud of yourselves. Over 50 different countries have adopted a form of the ADA.

You, the Congress, should be recognized for the many positive changes that have occurred since you passed the ADA: reduction in physical barriers. Everywhere one sees signs of a more accessible world. And that is rapidly getting better, as new office buildings and businesses are built in compliance with the law.

All of us have benefited from these changes in our physical and environmental stage, and the attitude of inclusion that accompanies these changes: curb-cuts and ramps designed to allow access for people with wheelchairs help parents with baby carriages, delivery people, mail carriers making their rounds and elderly people.

We now have access to information and technology usable by people with disabilities. Thanks to the ADA's clear call to equal access to the goods and services offered by public accommodations, people with disabilities are, more than ever before, finding it easier to privately and independently make purchases at retail stores such as pharmacies with accessible points-of-sale machines.

The Americans with Disabilities Act Still Has Much to Accomplish

Jim McKay

In the following selection, journalist Jim McKay addresses the shortcomings of the Americans with Disabilities Act (ADA). McKay recognizes that the ADA has enabled more people with significant mental and physical disabilities to live independently and have increased access to public places. However, he feels that the effects of exclusion and discrimination are still present, particularly in the employment arena. As examples McKay cites the extremely high unemployment rate of people with serious disabilities and the large percentage of individuals with disabilities who live below the poverty level. He states that the stereotypes about people with disabilities must be overcome in order to realize the full potential of the ADA.

In the 15 years since the Americans with Disabilities Act (ADA) was signed into law, there have been major improvements in making public places and services more accessible to people who live with physical impairments.

The law, intended to ensure equal rights for the disabled, has brought a host of changes in workplaces, transportation, communication and other areas. Companies must make reasonable attempts to accommodate workers with physical impairments, while buildings, transportation and other public facilities must be accessible to all.

The Shortcomings of the ADA

But even as the ADA is slowly driving changes enabling more people with significant mental and physical disabilities to live independently, the effects of exclusion are still felt, particularly

Jim McKay, "Americans with Disabilities Act: A Job Not Done (Yet)," *Pittsburgh Post-Gazette*, July 15, 2005. Copyright © 2008 *Pittsburgh Post-Gazette*. All rights reserved. Reprinted with permission.

in employment. That's because the ADA, which became law on July 26, 1990, is a significant yet imperfect piece of legislation, Mary A. Crossley, the new dean at the University of Pittsburgh School of Law [Pitt], said yesterday [July 14, 2005].

"I would not characterize it as a complete success, but I wouldn't characterize it as a failure. I think it is an important piece of legislation whose promise has not been fully realized," said Crossley, a scholar in disability and health law, who came to Pitt last week from the Florida State University College of Law.

"We still have a lot to do," Crossley said. "But [the ADA] is something I celebrate as an important recognition that people with disabilities are just like the rest of us, except they have some kind of disability, and they should not be excluded or segregated or face limitations that people without disabilities don't face."

Benefits Extend to Average Americans

Many of the architectural changes brought by the ADA have been embraced by a broader group of Americans. Sidewalk curb cuts and ramps designed to help people with disabilities, for example, are used by parents pushing strollers, workers delivering packages and travelers pulling suitcases on wheels.

Likewise, captioning on television designed for people who are deaf or hard of hearing is used by those not hearing impaired in noisy places like sports bars. And new building and product designs that are ADA compliant have universal appeal—an adjustable podium, a stairless entrance, a computer that can respond to voice commands or a voting machine that can read the ballot in multiple languages are enjoyed by everyone.

Employment Issues

But all those visible changes have yet to carry over where it perhaps matters most for people with disabilities—the job market.

The unemployment rate among people with serious disabilities is the highest of any group of Americans, no matter their education or qualifications, with roughly 70 percent of working-age people with significant disabilities not working—a level that has remained constant for about two decades, according to the U.S. Census Bureau.

"To a lot of us, that is disappointing," said Andrew Imparato, president and chief executive officer of the American Association of People with Disabilities.

Of 49.7 million Americans of all ages with disabilities, about two-thirds have disabilities that are classified as serious or significant.

The Census data is corroborated by a Harris survey commissioned by the National Organization on Disability that last year [2004] found only 35 percent of people with disabilities reported being employed either full or part time, compared with 78 percent of those who do not have disabilities.

Three times as many people with disabilities live in poverty—with annual household incomes below $15,000—than people without disabilities, the survey found. They are also more likely to need transportation and to go without needed health care.

It should be no surprise, then, that people with disabilities are less likely to socialize, eat out or attend religious services than their non-disabled counterparts. Only 34 percent of those surveyed said they were very satisfied with their lives.

Joyce Bender, an executive recruiter from Pittsburgh who has made a national business out of finding jobs for qualified people with disabilities, called the high unemployment among people with disabilities a "national failure."

For Bender, who discovered she had epilepsy 21 years ago after a hemorrhage in a movie house, the ADA means she need not disclose in an employment application that her seizure disorder is controlled with medication.

But she said employers 15 years after the act's passage still regularly ask her to detail what disabilities her employment clients have—a question that is barred by the act as discriminatory.

"We still have a long way to go," said Bender, who operates employment services in 13 states and expects to hire 100 new employees with significant disabilities this year.

Beyond the ADA

The problem, of course, is bigger than a legal statute. Although some people blame the ADA for failing to curb high unemployment, Imparato said that is not quite fair.

The ADA did not—and was not meant to—create all of the employment and training programs that would be needed to lift up people with disabilities who are undereducated so they could be competitive in job searches.

The simple fact is, there are people with disabilities who are trained and qualified yet don't even get a chance to compete for jobs. Imparato said employers have not gone after people with disabilities in the same way they compete to find qualified women or minority applications.

"That is the kind of thing I'm hoping will change," he said. "I think of it as almost generational. My children are going to be less likely to discriminate than my generation, and hopefully their children will be less likely to discriminate than they."

Much of the continued discrimination can be traced to stereotypes about people with disabilities, said Clifford Payne, a vice president of Accessibility Development Associates Inc., a Pittsburgh company that advises business, government and other clients on how to cope with the ADA.

"The good thing is that the ADA has really changed society. Go to any shopping mall and you will see people there independently in wheel chairs, with their friends and family groups. You didn't used to see that," Payne said.

Some employers, he said, continue to drag their feet over making physical accommodations to help people with disabilities. But Payne believes negative attitudes are a larger issue.

"The biggest obstacle is the stereotypes about people with disabilities, that people with disabilities will be more expensive to hire, that once I hire them I can't fire them, and my personal favorite, I don't want to bring a crazy person into my workplace," Payne said.

"People with mental health disabilities face an incredible amount of prejudice and that includes people who take medicine for things like depression."

Court Cases

Since the ADA's inception, there have been several court decisions, including a few by the U.S. Supreme Court, that have narrowed the class of people who are protected by the law.

In a 2002 case involving Toyota Motor Manufacturing, the court ruled that an assembly line worker with carpal tunnel syndrome who was fired because of her attendance record was not entitled to protection under the act because it was not clear that she had substantial impairment of any major life activity.

A similar rationale was used in a 1999 case in which a truck driver for a supermarket chain was fired for not meeting visual standards. The company refused to rehire him even after he obtained a waiver from the standards.

Also in 1999, the Supreme Court found that severely myopic twins who had unsuccessfully sought pilot jobs with United Airlines were not actually disabled because their vision could be corrected by eyeglasses.

Those decisions have led some advocates of people with disabilities to call on Congress to legislatively update the ADA to counter the negative effects of court decisions and make it more inclusive.

Crossley, Pitt's new law school dean, said amendments to the act may be necessary but she suggested there are other steps to consider, including gains in education and the passage of time, that could further help to end discrimination and bring people with disabilities into society as equal partners.

"Most of us, if we live long enough, will some day find an individual with disabilities in our families."

Murderers with Mental Disabilities Are Not Executed Disproportionately

Dudley Sharp

In the following selection, Dudley Sharp reviews the evaluation process required to designate an individual as mentally retarded in the legal system. Sharp feels that there are multiple fallacies present in the death penalty debate, including that mentally incompetent people are being executed. The decision to execute a criminal is based on a full review of the issues and the individual's competency, argues Sharp. Therefore a disproportionate number of mentally retarded individuals are not being executed, despite what others may argue. Dudley Sharp is a member of Justice for All, a criminal justice reform group that focuses largely on the victims of violent crimes.

Much of the presentation regarding excluding the execution of the mentally retarded has been either highly deceptive or lacking in a clinical foundation or both.

We hope this essay helps to correct that.

Some say that we mustn't execute people who do not know right from wrong and who lack understanding [of] the severity of their crimes. The reality is that we have not been executing such people for decades, because current law doesn't allow it.

Currently, during pre-trial, trial and appeals, the law provides evaluation for mental competency—and such an evaluation requires that the defendant understand the consequences of their actions, that they must be able to constructively participate in their own defense and that they understand the na-

Dudley Sharp, "Mental Retardation and the Death Penalty," *Justice for All*, October 18, 2001. Reproduced by permission.

ture of their punishment. Furthermore, mental capability is one of the many issues that a jury might consider when establishing mitigation which may dictate a sentence less than death. Quite simply, only mentally competent capital murderers can face either execution or life in prison.

And that is appropriate.

Illustrations of Inconsistency

Here is an example of the type of obfuscation and ignorance that is often seen within this issue.

Death penalty opponents state that Texas has executed 6 mentally retarded capital murderers. Those executed are defined as mentally retarded by their IQ numbers. First, mental health professionals state that IQ measurements alone cannot establish mental retardation. So states that solely use that standard to exclude a possible death sentence have used an improper standard and those who declare people mentally retarded simply by IQ numbers are equally incorrect.

Those Texas six are called mentally retarded because they allegedly had a measured IQ of below 70—a standard below which some establish mental retardation. First, death penalty opponents will often list only the lowest recorded general IQ numbers of the murderer and intentionally withhold other tests which recorded much higher numbers. Such opponents also fail to note that there is a margin of error of plus or minus 10 points within that IQ evaluation, meaning that only those who score below a 60 on their maximum IQ test can establish mental retardation by using those numbers.

Furthermore, general IQ is not even relevant to the evaluations. Only performance IQ, which attempts to measure a person's abilities to function effectively under real world situations, is the relevant issue, if one improperly wishes to just "go by the numbers." Again, those states and advocates who use only general IQ evaluations have misunderstood or improperly applied that qualification.

Actual Executions Lacking

And based on that analysis, as well as a review of the case facts, such opponents cannot support their claims that Texas has executed even a single mentally retarded murderer. I suggest that may likely be the case in other states, as well.

A case example:

During Texas' last legislative session, in the spring of 2001, supporters of HB236 [House bill 236], a bill to ban execution of the mentally retarded, held a public rally at the capitol in Austin and invoked the case of Mario Marquez, executed in 1995, as one of those 6 cases and stated that Marquez was exactly that kind of murderer which HB236 was designed to protect. Supporters of that bill could not have provided a better case for Texans to oppose this bill and for Governor [Rick] Perry to veto it.

Marquez was angry that his wife was leaving him, so, in retaliation, he murdered his wife's 14-year-old niece, Rachel and his 18-year-old estranged wife, Rebecca. They were beaten and raped . . . then strangled to death. . . . Marquez then waited for his mother-in-law, to return home, beat and sexually assaulted her—then presented the two brutalized bodies of the two girls to her—as trophies for his anger.

There is little doubt but that he was also going to murder his mother-in-law, but Marquez's continued assault on her was interrupted and he fled from the scene.

Marquez's performance IQ was measured at 75—16 points above the minimum number required to establish that arbitrary "mental retardation" standard, using the plus or minus 10 point variable. And Marquez's life and crimes, spanning many years, fully support that Marquez knew exactly what he was doing.

When given the facts of specific crimes, like Marquez's, many would agree with the jury—that such mentally competent, guilty capital murderers should face the death penalty, as a sentencing option. . . .

Other Discussion Points

1. Many argue strenuously to halt execution of the "mentally retarded," yet they do nothing to properly define what "mentally retarded" means in a fashion reflecting a full understanding of the issues, much less do they discuss the premeditation, planning and consideration which the alleged "mentally retarded" murderers so often invested in the murders. A full accounting should be demanded in any public policy discussion, and

2. Many argue strenuously against a death penalty option for the mentally retarded, but they fail to tell us why such individuals should not be subject to execution, but should be subject to a life sentence. Is the murderer any less guilty or culpable for one sentence than the other? A jury may decide that the murderer deserves a lesser sentence, because of any mitigation which may be reflected by competency issues, but that decision is best made by the jury, which has all the case facts before it. Much of the effort to exempt the "mentally retarded" from execution can best be described as another effort to reduce the application of a proper sentencing option by those who oppose executions under all circumstances.

3. In establishing a below 70 IQ number as the threshold for withholding a death sentence option, several important issues are often neglected a) the previously discussed issue of both the 10 point variable and the performance IQ issues, as well as b) when the IQ test was taken. If the test was taken after an arrest, then there is a strong likelihood that the arrested party would do everything possible to score as low as possible, as a self-preservation issue. This would negate the reliability of the test. And as you can never be sure about that issue, under those circumstances, then other means will have to be used to establish competency and c) IQ tests' re-

sults, with the same individual, can vary greatly over time, well outside any 10 point variable. This directly goes to those states which have standards that say the test must have been administered prior to age 18. Both education and experience can increase IQ's over time. Therefore, that prior to age 18 rule may allow a competent murderer to escape proper punishment, only because of an arbitrary and capricious standard, which had no relevance at the time of the murder. And, again, the distinction between general and performance IQ come into play, as well as all the other variables and limitations.

First, Determine Competency

That is why the current system, as it now exists, is the best. Determine competency pre-trial. Relive those issues again, at trial and on appeal. Establish if the defendant knew right from wrong, if the defendant can constructively participate in their own defense and establish if they understand the nature of their punishment. And review those issues, again, on appeal.

That appears to be the most responsible and honest method of reviewing these cases and issues. Any other method is more arbitrary and capricious. To date, there is nothing to indicate that a better system has been presented. If you review those state statutes which ban the death penalty for the "mentally retarded," you will find that virtually all of them have some problems which make their death penalty statutes more arbitrary and capricious and which do not reflect a full appreciation of the issues. In effect, what many of those states have done is to pass laws which will allow fully competent murderers to escape the most appropriate punishment consideration. Remember, these statutes are specifically directed against the death sentence, not lesser sentences.

And finally, to address the cruel and unusual punishment question. Based upon current law and legal opinion, at the US Supreme Court level, execution of the mentally retarded is not cruel and unusual punishment. But, in making such judgments, we should rely on a full review of the issues and not base our conclusions on emotion and incomplete and inaccurate presentations.

Criminals with Mental Disabilities Should Be Exempt from Capital Punishment

Laurence Armand French

In the following selection, Laurence Armand French discusses the clinical and legal background of the death penalty for mentally disabled offenders. French asserts his belief that individuals with mental disabilities do not have the same mental resources as average adults and will never be in a position to be fully responsible for their actions. Based on this supposition, it is cruel and unusual punishment for mentally retarded offenders to be put to death for criminal behavior. Laurence French is the director of the psychology program in the Department of Social Sciences at Western New Mexico University.

An obvious cultural lag long existing between the United States and its European and North American allies surrounds the death penalty. The 2002 U.S. Supreme Court ruling, *Atkins v. Virginia*, finally outlawed the practice of "death qualifying" mentally retarded (MR) offenders, a practice long abandoned by other democracies. . . . The mentally retarded . . . have diminished cognitive capacity due to birth defects or accidents and brain insults prior to the age of 18. Unlike adolescents, the mentally retarded are not likely to ever correct their status of diminished responsibility. This fact has long been recognized, leading to the well-intended but ill-fated sterilization laws enacted in much of the U.S. during the 20th century.

Ironically, while clinical disciplines, including psychology, have made significant contributions to the current MR and

Laurence Armand French, "Mental Retardation and the Death Penalty: The Clinical and Legal Legacy," *Federal Probation*, vol. 69, no. 1, June 2005. http://www.uscourts.gov/fedprob.

juvenile offender cases before the high court, they have also contributed historically to the now questionable practices of eugenics, a foundation for the most severe societal sanction— the death penalty for mentally retarded offenders. Interestingly, the U.S. Supreme Court based its death penalty decisions not on international consensus but rather on "national consensus." But once this means test was met, the Court used clinical evidence to support its ban on "death qualifying" the mentally retarded. The current foundation for the June 2002 U.S. Supreme Court decision (*Atkins v. Virginia*) is rooted in the new neurological research available within the past 15 years and represented by current clinical assessment tools, including the *Diagnostic and Statistical Manual of Mental Disorders* (DSM-IV-TR).

Defining Mental Retardation

The *Atkins* decision reads: "Execution of criminals who were mentally retarded held to constitute cruel and unusual punishment in violation of Federal Constitution's Eighth Amendment." Essentially the Court felt that the execution of the mentally retarded would not measurably contribute to either deterrence or retribution within the U.S. criminal justice system. The Court also noted that mentally retarded defendants face a greater risk of wrongful execution before the judicial system and therefore warrant special protection. In *Atkins*, the U.S. Supreme Court noted that the evolving standards of decency within the country now prohibit the execution of people who are mentally retarded. The scientific basis for this decision cites the standards set forth by both the American Association on Mental Retardation (AAMR) and the American Psychiatric Association that MR is basically defined as 1) significant subaverage general intellectual functioning, 2) concurrent with deficits in adaptive functioning, and 3) occurring before age 18.

Clearly the introduction of clinical elements in the death penalty argument is significant—but not new. Even then, jurisdictions such as Texas continue to defy *Atkins* by challenging the clinical definition of mental retardation, bringing to the forefront the marked, and often contravening, differences between the legal and mental health disciplines and their respective definitions of the situation. Contributing to this dilemma concerning a concise measure of mental retardation are the conflicting definitions offered by two separate organizations: the American Association on Mental Retardation and the American Psychiatric Association (APA). In *Atkins* the U.S. Supreme Court used the 1992 AAMR definition:

> Mental retardation refers to substantial limitations in present functioning. It is characterized by significantly subaverage intellectual functioning, existing concurrently with related limitations in two or more of the following applicable adaptive skill areas: communication, self-care, home living, social skills, community use, self-direction, health and safety, functional academics, leisure, and work. Mental retardation manifests itself before age 18.

The American Psychiatric Association definition that is listed in the DSM-IV-TR offers variable IQ ranges for each of the four categories, while also noting that MR has numerous etiologies and: "may be seen as a final common pathway of various pathological processes that affect the functioning of the central nervous system." Here, Mild Mental Retardation, one of five codes within the MR classification diagnosis, is listed as an IQ range of 50 to 55 to approximately 70. Accordingly, a seventy IQ reflects two standard deviations from the normative IQ of 100 or a statistically significant departure from the norm as stated in the Atkins decision. Texas continues to challenge the measurement of the IQ range requisite for a diagnosis of mental retardation in its attempt to continue to death qualify offenders with low-range intelligence.

The IQ Controversy

The role of psychology in the classification of intelligence, and hence legal competence, goes back to the origin of intelligence measurement itself—the Binet Simon developed in France in the early 1900s by psychologist Alfred Binet and physician Theodore Simon. However, it was the U.S. version—the Stanford-Binet [devised by Stanford University professor Lewis Terman]—that made dramatic claims relevant to its power to predict deviant and/or criminal behaviors, hence paving the way for legal sanctions directed toward those labeled "subaverage. . . ."

To Terman, general intelligence testing provided sufficient evidence to evaluate and label serious deviants in society. Included here was the implicit plan for social control, including the elimination of the mentally deficient through institutionalization and sterilization. Indeed, the influence of Francis Galton's eugenics coupled with Terman's U.S. version of the Binet was so profound that by 1926, 23 states had enacted mental retardation sterilization laws, 18 of those providing for mandatory sterilization of those classified as being mentally deficient, including habitual criminals. In 1927, the U.S. Supreme Court upheld involuntary sterilization in *Buck v. Bell*. A recent study by faculty at Johns Hopkins University compares eugenic sterilization in both the United States and Germany from 1930 until 1945. While the numbers of U.S. forced sterilizations pale in comparison with the 360,000 to 375,000 affected by this practice during Nazi rule (this number not including those exterminated during the Holocaust), some 40,000 persons were involuntarily sterilized in America during this period. Involuntary sterilization ended in the United States, at both the state and federal levels, during the Civil Rights era of the 1960s, when it was realized that those most likely to be subjected to this practice were poor minorities, notably African Americans and Native Americans.

The race/class and IQ controversy continued into the 1970s and 1980s with the *Larry P. v. Riles* case. The *Larry P.* challenge, filed in 1971, was a class-action suit representing African-American children and youth labeled as being EMR (educable mentally retarded) by the San Francisco Public Schools and subsequently placed in special education classes. The suit claimed that flawed IQ assessments resulted in a disproportionate number of minority children being placed in "educable mentally retarded classes." The petitioners contended that this process violates Title IV of the 1964 Civil Rights Act, the 1973 Rehabilitation Act, and Public Law 94–142—the 1975 Education for All Handicapped Children Act (EAHCA of 1975). One of the petitioners, the Bay Area Association of Black Psychologists, sought a ban on IQ testing, especially single measure indicators of general intelligence. The Association argued that existing IQ tests were not adequately standardized to reflect minority subcultures in the United States, hence resulting in these students having a greater likelihood of being placed in stigmatizing special education curriculum that, in turn, led to a greater school drop-out rate and a marked disadvantage in the job market once they left school. French noted that the mechanism of testing stigma is tantamount to *blaming the victim*, a self-fulfilling prophecy whereby minorities, including the mentally retarded, are blamed for their poor test results and therefore become labeled as deviant.

The *Larry P.* case worked its way through the California courts and into the federal appeals courts, ending with the Circuit Court of Appeals in 1984. The result was an agreement that no assessment of ability would rest on a single instrument. Equally compelling was the move to better norm subsequent versions of existing instruments as well as to include other measures of mental retardation, such as medical etiologies, life histories and the like in order to rule out class, ethnic, and racial factors.

Deinstitutionalization

Another factor leading to the execution of the mentally retarded was the movement toward deinstitutionalization that began in the 1960s with the advent of new psychotropic medications and the movement toward community mental health facilities. Interestingly, the deinstitutionalization process in the United States was initiated in the prisons and only later involved facilities for the mentally retarded. Two major U.S. Supreme Court cases occurred in the 1980s—*Youngberg v. Romeo*, 1982; and *City of Cleburne v. Cleburne Living Center*, 1985)—setting the stage for the current U.S. Supreme Court decision. Additionally, the *Larry P. v. Riles* case challenged the reliability and validity of intelligence testing, especially among minorities challenging Terman's faith in the ultimate power of IQ tests. Even then the *Atkins* ruling allows the state to determine how mentally retarded offenders are to be assessed and measured. Part of this dilemma can be traced to the fact that *Larry P. v. Riles* was not appealed to the U.S. Supreme Court. . . .

In 1977, in *Halderman v. Pennhurst*, a federal Court ordered the first closing of a U.S. mental health facility. In its decision, the Court determined that confinement and isolation of retarded residents at the Pennhurst State School constituted segregation. Moreover, the Court cited the state school for not abiding to the minimal treatment standards set out in *Wyatt [v. Stickney]* [1971, which addressed the rights of involuntarily confined mentally retarded clients]. The state of Pennsylvania appealed the decision all the way to the U.S. Supreme Court, setting the stage for the 1982 *Youngberg [v. Romeo]* decision.

Both the *Youngberg* and *Cleburne* cases had unintended consequences that unwittingly fueled the mentally retarded death penalty controversy in addition to their manifest intent of improving the lives of the mentally retarded population in the United States. The *Youngberg* case was significant in that the U.S. Supreme Court based this decision on lower court rulings and in contrast to its 1926 *Buck v. Bell* decision sanctioning eugenics via sterilization of the mentally retarded. The *Youngberg* case addressed the *Wyatt 71, 72, 74* standards relevant to the involuntary confinement of the mentally retarded. In *Youngberg* the U.S. Supreme Court nationalized these standards across the country.

Essentially the U.S. Supreme Court looked at the case of Nicholas Romeo, an involuntary resident of Pennhurst State School and Hospital, relevant to his Fourteenth Amendment rights. The Court held that involuntarily committed mentally retarded residents have a constitutional right to habilitation and training. Indeed, the U.S. Supreme Court explicitly stated that involuntarily committed persons afflicted with mental retardation have the same rights to due process as do prison inmates, including habeas corpus petitions: "If it is cruel and unusual punishment to hold convicted criminals in unsafe conditions, it must be unconstitutional to confine the involuntarily committed—who may not be punished at all—in unsafe conditions."

Rights of the Disabled

The *Youngberg* decision states that mentally disabled people cannot be deprived of the following interests that are clearly recognized as constitutionally required for institutional care:

1. Reasonable care and safety.
2. Freedom from bodily restraints.
3. Adequate food, shelter, clothing, and medical care.
4. Those liberty interests to which convicted criminals are entitled.
5. Adequate training or habilitation to ensure the enjoyment of liberty.

The *Youngberg* ruling touched upon a number of critical clinical and legal areas affecting both institutional care (quality of care; habilitation and treatment; aftercare) and community placement (mainstreaming into public group homes). Many states found it too expensive to maintain their state schools and psychiatric hospitals under these conditions, resulting in the release of significant numbers of mentally retarded and mentally ill (MI) clients into communities that were ill-prepared for the intensity of their care. Ironically, prisons and jails now became the home of inadequately treated MR and dual diagnosed MR/MI individuals. The clinical safety net was not adequate at that time and still is deficient in many states, leading to long backlogs of never-treated mentally retarded individuals, making them all the more susceptible to criminal adjudication.

Resistance Against Group Homes

Community resistance to group homes led to the second major U.S. Supreme Court decision regarding the care of the MR. In the 1985 *City of Cleburne v. Cleburne Living Center* case, the Court ruled that mental retardation in itself does not determine a quasi-suspect class and therefore does not warrant special legal rights beyond those afforded all citizens under the Equal Protection Clause of the Fourteenth Amendment. By the same token, the Court struck down zoning ordinances that may discriminate against group homes for mentally retarded clients. This ruling proved to be a mixed blessing for advocates of deinstitutionalization. While the ruling removed a serious obstacle to strategically located group homes for this population, it also denied these mainstreamed clients additional special considerations that may have been available if they were afforded "quasi-suspect" classification, such as is extended to the mentally ill. A major consequence of this ruling was the changing of mental retardation from an Axis I major clinical syndrome to Axis II, beginning with the 1987 *Diagnostic and Statistical Manual* (DSM-III-R) and in all subsequent versions.

The DSM and the Criminal Adjudication Process

Axis I disorders, . . . offer defendants substantial license regarding mitigating circumstances. This is especially critical in the two-phase adjudication process articulated in the U.S. Supreme Court's reinstatement of the death penalty in 1976, following its 1972 *Furman v. Georgia* ruling on the death sentence as being unconstitutional as administered up to that time. The advent of the DSM-III in 1980 greatly aided forensic psychology and psychiatry by providing a scientific multi-axle model of clinical definitions based on the World Health Organization's International Classifications of Diseases (ICD). This provided for a more objective marriage between the clinical and legal disciplines in civil, criminal and juvenile court hearings with the generally accepted understanding that Axis I major clinical disorders and/or syndromes could be presented as mitigating circumstances in order to challenge aggravating circumstances. On the other hand, it was generally held that Axis II disorders were not to be considered significant factors that could override aggravating circumstances. At the time of the DSM-III, personality disorders were the only category in Axis II.

But following the U.S. Supreme Court's 1985 *Cleburne* decision that the mentally retarded did not share the same special protected class as the mentally ill, MR classifications were relegated to Axis II, beginning with the 1987 DSM-III-R. This shift in classification now made mentally retarded defendants "death qualified" even under the two-tier adjudication death qualifying system approved by the U.S. Supreme Court and used from 1976 until the present. It would be interesting to know how many, if any, MR defendants were spared being "death qualified" between 1976 and 1985. At any rate, the resulting separation of the MR class from the same legal protection held by the mentally ill (MI) class was seen by many as an unfortunate unintended consequence of the *Cleburne* decision. . . .

The American Psychological Association filed an amicus brief in the *Roper v. Simmons* case before the U.S. Supreme Court. The brief supported banning the death penalty for youth, presenting recent psychological research that indicates that youth are more impulsive and take more risks than adults, make more immature decisions, fail to resist peer influence and are more susceptible to coercion and false confessions: "The brief includes recent brain-imaging research on brain functioning that suggests an average brain continues to develop through the teen years, particularly in areas that control decision-making." Clearly, as the Supreme Court ultimately agreed in *Roper v. Simmons*, the arguments for diminished capacity also apply to the mentally retarded and youth. There is clear scientific evidence that these classes of individuals do not have the same mental resources and capacity as adults when it comes to full criminal responsibility—the standard which provides the basis for mens tea and hence the justification for society's ultimate sanction—death.

CHAPTER 3

Education for People with Disabilities

Chapter Preface

In 1973 the U.S. Congress passed legislation called the Rehabilitation Act. This bill primarily focused on providing job opportunities and training to disabled adults; however, included in this act was Section 504, which required federally funded schools to provide "free appropriate public education" to students with disabilities. The act in its entirety was considered a triumph of advocacy by disability rights groups. However, this triumph sparked educational debates that have continued for fifty years.

Educators, administrators, and parents express often conflicting opinions on the most beneficial manner in which to educate children with disabilities. A large part of this debate has arisen from the diverse, or heterogeneous, nature of the disabled. Overarching policies put in place to aid the majority of disabled students may be ineffective for others. For example, some disabled individuals thrive in specialized classroom settings separated from the average students. Some school districts, however, have phased out segregated special education in favor of mainstream learning, in which students are placed among the general school population. This broad stroke approach to education angers the factions who support specialized classrooms that were initiated to provide the individual care that many children with special needs require to learn life and academic skills. Joining in the debate are the parents of average students who oppose classrooms that mainstream nondisabled children with special needs children because they feel it will impact the average child's education negatively. All sides in the debate offer classroom studies, anecdotal evidence, and case reports to support their positions.

Further debate focuses on the amount of funding required to create and maintain educational opportunities for special needs children. Schools with limited funds may spend a disproportionate amount of money on special education, which necessitates decreased spending in other areas such as art and music. This type of budgeting often causes resentment in parents of nondisabled children who view this practice as unfair. However, parents of disabled students often feel that their children have a right to a core educational plan that works effectively for them regardless of the cost. Funding is an issue that continues to be debated by parents and educators. The viewpoints in this chapter further illustrate the complex issues related to educating students with disabilities.

Separate Classrooms Are the Best Environment for Children with Disabilities

Mary Sharp

In the following selection, Mary Sharp, a physician and mother of a son with disabilities, disagrees with the concept that mainstreaming in the regular classroom is the best alternative for children with disabilities. Sharp notes that while some children may flourish in an inclusion classroom setting, specialized education classrooms are constructed to provide the individual care that many children with special needs require to learn life and academic skills.

How you think you should behave as a parent and how you think your child should be taught come out of the same deep place inside. Schooling is a very emotional topic. We all know stories of horrible things going on in classrooms, and there is much righteous fodder for the educational reform movement. But rigid thinking about a school's structure erupts from the same dark source as rigid thinking about a successful family.

It gets even more emotional when you throw in disability. With the abandonment of the developmentally disabled by the medical system, the societal responsibility has been shifted to the school systems. A lot of good has come of this. Special services can most conveniently and effectively be served up in this setting. What an experienced special education teacher or occupational therapist or autism specialist has to say about a

Mary Sharp, "Schooling," *An Unexpected Joy: The Gift of Parenting a Challenging Child*, Colorado Springs, CO: Pinon Press, 2003, pp. 102–107. Copyright © 2003 by Mary Sharp. All rights reserved. Reproduced by permission.

problem is much more likely to be helpful than what your physician has to say. There is no disputing the advantages to our kids from the Americans with Disabilities Act (ADA) and the development of services and accessibility that has resulted from this legislation.

Resentment Toward Special Needs Children

I am always shocked when I run into resentment toward special needs kids and the amount of money spent on their education. I am not aware of people resenting speech rehab services for their elderly stroke relatives or post-closed-head injury rehab for young adults after their skiing, diving, or auto accidents. The public is quite naive about medical insurance. Many people in my state are so used to extraordinary coverage that they think of their insurance cards like a charge card, with the bill going to someone else. The notion of insurance money being a pooled, collective resource is lost on them.

A more visible form of pooled money is the public-school dollar. This is probably because of the election of local school boards and public voting on school millage issues. Parents feel they have more control over this money and are therefore more vigilant stewards. So they resent the extra dollars it takes to educate disabled kids. They see it as money not being spent on their kids. They are unaware of the shift of this responsibility out of their medical dollar—which they view unrealistically—into the more visible public-school dollar. The idea that these dependent individuals will otherwise end up on welfare, another pooled money pot, is lost on many of them. Basically, the biggest bang for the buck is the money spent on schooling these kids. It will result in less money being spent from the other pots.

Effective Inclusion Programs

The passage of the ADA [in 1990] resulted from years of persistent, effective lobbying by disabled individuals and their families. Part of that early activist movement was the radical notion of inclusion. The concept of least restrictive environment was introduced and determined to be an important goal in meeting the needs of special education students.

This was good. It brought many problems out of the closet. All kids benefit enormously from effective inclusion programs. Both the special-needs child and the typical child benefit, as they do from anything that increases healthy diversity in their classroom.

A few years ago, Cory was part of Nic's [the author's son] special-ed classroom. They spent about two years together. Then it was decided that Cory would do better in a mainstream classroom. He has flourished with the help of a paraprofessional (not a certified teacher, but a person skilled in assisting special-needs students), some great teachers, and a good group of kids. It is tradition in their school at Halloween to parade through all the classrooms. As a visiting parent, I enjoy watching the progression from sweet little five-year-old princesses and fairies to sixth-grade boys pushing the rules as hard as they can, dressed in as bloody and macabre costumes as they think they can get away with. About two years ago, I was in Nic's room, watching the parade. I was pleased to see Cory come parading through, dressed as a muscle man. His foam rubber muscles rippled masculinely and he was clearly enjoying himself. His former classmates stood up and started to chant, "Cory, Cory, Cory." They were so proud of him. It was like the victor had returned. Cory had gone out into the big time and made it. I don't think Rocky [the prizefighter movie character] could have felt any better.

Ineffective Inclusion Programs

Ineffective inclusion programs are another matter altogether. When they're bad, everyone loses. But in too many schools, the trend is to push everyone into the mainstream. When that happens, an individual assessment of the child's needs isn't considered, and inclusion is hyped as a goal for all special-needs children.

Nic did not benefit from inclusion. The worst year of his school career was the year he spent in a mainstream classroom. And this was with the cards stacked in his favor. He had a marvelous teacher, whom he knew from his PPI (pre-primary impaired) classroom. He had a loving and experienced parapro [paraprofessional aide]. The parents of the other kids in his class bent over backward to include him. It was simply too much for Nic. There was too much noise, activity, and visual stimulation. All that enrichment was right for the regular kids, but it was toxic for him.

I have two concerns about mainstreaming. The first is what I call malicious mainstreaming. Parents who are still in denial about their child's prognosis commit this. They insist on mainstreaming because they mistake the process of role modeling provided by the other students for a normalizing process. When a year goes by and there is no change in their child, they think the teacher has done something wrong or someone is to blame.

My other concern has to do with the basic nature of humans. My son has known he was different from the get-go. He has communicated this to me in many ways, most of them nonverbal. When you put a child who is profoundly different in with a bunch of fully equipped kids, everyone knows what's going on. If the children have been brought up well, they are polite and practice acts of inclusion as they are able to. Many are very kind. If they have not been brought up well, they can be cruel. Neither of these is an ideal environment because both preclude the development of a real peer group. No one likes to be around kids who've been treated with kid gloves all the time. They tend to be brats. In the opposite direction, any report on school violence will summarize the worst-case effects of taunting, teasing, and other peer cruelty.

A Contained Classroom May Be the Best Answer

I believe a critical mass of time spent with real peers allows true friendships to grow. This is as good as it gets. We found this in Nic's contained classroom.

A good teacher uses these real relationships to teach. Renee, Nic's current teacher, is the gold standard in my book. My son knows about "showing heart" and "giving zingers" because these behaviors are illustrated and discussed in his classroom every day. Renee is able to make these principles concrete.

The continuity we have been blessed with has allowed a real classroom culture to develop. This in turn benefits the younger kids who come into the room. For my son to be a role model for a seven-year-old is huge. He sees himself as competent and feels pride. This is true growth. It helps interrupt the cycle of constant dependence that so many of these kids suffer from. When they're around the regular kids, they are never fast enough or smart enough or acceptable enough. That is an exhausting way to live. If we didn't have a contained classroom, I don't believe these trusting relationships could have developed.

Also, we have a social life. We don't have to apologize for bizarre and irritating behavior at the movies. Birthday parties are as much fun for the parents as the kids because we can talk to people who understand our day-to-day trials.

The children in Nic's class are remarkable. They show pure and simple tolerance of diversity. They are sib-like with each other, which means they can be joyful with each other and then turn around and give each other a hard time. The kid gloves are off, and they're on as even a playing field as they'll ever get. This is a much more balanced environment for them to grow in. Mainstreaming cannot provide this kind of intimacy.

If Nic did not have a brother and sister who gave him grief, wrestled with him, and told him what was cool and what was not, I'd feel the need for some mainstream contact. But he does have these paragons of popular culture in his life, and I am thankful for that.

Nic is "with it" enough now to follow some fads. He may not get the point of the fad, like that you could play a game with Pokemon cards, but he knew the cards were cool and he enjoyed having some because they made him feel cool. Currently, he's obsessed with Harry Potter.

As Nic gets older, the discrepancy between him and his same-age peers becomes more glaring. That's hard. I worry about other children exploiting him when he goes off to middle school. But he has to go to middle school. He's almost the tallest one at his elementary school, and soon he's going to need to shave. I am confident I will survive the transition, and as with every other step he's taken, in addition to the stress, there will be unanticipated victories and treasures.

Inclusive Education Is Beneficial to Students with Disabilities and Without

Kathy Flores

In the following selection, behavior specialist Kathy Flores discusses the benefits of inclusive education—a program that mixes children with special needs and those without. Flores feels that inclusive education is not easy or inexpensive, but benefits all children. However, she notes that in order for inclusive education to work effectively, the teachers and staff must be trained and have ongoing support, and the parents and students must be taught inclusive attitudes.

Valerie is passionate about music, loves parties, and enjoys hanging out with friends. She's a doting big sister and an avid [San Francisco] Giants [baseball] fan.

She's also severely disabled. A disease called Rhett Syndrome robs her body of all voluntary movement except for minimal use of one hand. She eats with feeding tubes and communicates with a voice output device.

With the help of adaptive technology, Valerie is performing on grade level in regular classes in a San Francisco public school. Her mom, Audrey deChadenedes, fought hard to get her into regular classes. "I wanted Valerie to be part of the community at school and feel comfortable in the world," she says. "When I was growing up, I never saw disabled kids, and that wasn't right. The world is full of all kinds of people, and they all have value. Kids should learn that."

Inclusive Education

Federal law says students with disabilities should be included with other kids as much as possible, but many children with

Kathy Flores, "Special Needs, 'Mainstream' Classroom," *Children's Advocate*, January–February 2003. Reproduced by permission.

disabilities have been separated in special education classes. Prompted by a group of parents, the San Francisco Unified School District has been pursuing an ambitious inclusion initiative since 1993—so far nearly half of the district's schools are participating.

Other districts are also moving toward greater inclusion. The Los Angeles Unified School District has been working on inclusive education to implement a 1996 court order stemming from a parent lawsuit.

For some children, like Valerie, inclusion means spending all day in "mainstream" classrooms. Others study core subjects in special education classes and join mainstream art, music, or physical education classes. "There is no one model of inclusive education," says Deborah McKnight, San Francisco's interim executive director of special education. Special education, she says, "is a service, not a place. It is about meeting the needs of students, whatever those needs may be."

The Benefits: For Kids with Disabilities

Here are three examples:

Cruz, who is autistic, is in a regular first-grade class with the assistance of a paraprofessional aide. His teacher's special picture cues, the reading of stories about social situations, and participation in class meetings all help him learn appropriate behavior. He is happy in school and making friends.

Tony, who is developmentally delayed and has severe behavior problems, was mainstreamed in a drama class. With the teacher modeling acceptance, the other children helped Tony follow directions and participate. His behavior improved, he made friends, and according to his grateful mother, had the best school year of his life.

Patrick, who is deaf, attended an elementary school where he received some of his instruction in classes for deaf students, the rest in mainstream classes with the aid of an interpreter. He learned to relate to and make friends with both hearing and deaf people.

"Inclusion also results in greater academic gains," says Lois Jones, executive director of Parents Helping Parents of San Francisco, "and, just as importantly, language gains for children with disabilities."

The Benefits for Other Kids

Greater understanding: Aruna Subramanian, inclusion specialist at San Francisco's Cesar Chavez School, says, "Parents learn the benefits by watching their children interacting. Parents of nondisabled children see that their kids' learning is enhanced by the presence of the disabled kids."

Kim Lind has a student with Down Syndrome in her fourth-grade class at West Portal School in San Francisco. His aide is there only part of the day, so the other kids help him when he needs help. "Sometimes I think that the other kids in the class get even more out of it than he does," she says. "They learn how to treat other people who aren't just like them."

Better teaching: "You have to learn to be a better teacher to teach different kinds of kids," Subramanian adds. "It makes learning better for all kids." Including students with disabilities can prompt teachers to use more creative methods, such as cooperative learning and differential instruction (teaching to children's different learning styles), which benefit all their students.

What Makes It Work?

Commitment of school leadership. "If the principal isn't cooperative, you're out of luck," says J.C. Flores, mother of two autistic children in Los Angeles. Inclusion works in schools like West Portal, where everyone, not just special education teachers, is expected to share responsibility for educating children with disabilities.

Specially trained staff. In each San Francisco school with an inclusion program, an inclusion specialist is on staff to work with classroom teachers. In addition, many children with disabilities need a specially trained aide with them in the classroom.

Adapting the curriculum. Tiffany Kendall, inclusion specialist at West Portal, helps classroom teachers make modifications for students with special needs: A student with fine motor problems uses a marker and whiteboard instead of paper and pencil. A student with severe reading problems has a peer tutor read to him and listens to books on CDs. A student with cerebral palsy uses an adaptive keyboard. A teacher rings a bell to cue students with Attention Deficit Disorder to prepare for a transition.

At Cesar Chavez School, says Subramanian, a developmentally delayed student in fourth grade "wanted to work in the same math book on the same page as the other kids, but he didn't know how to do multiplication. So we let him add the numbers instead."

Training and time for collaboration. Most classroom teachers need training and ongoing support to effectively teach such a wide range of learners. They also need time to meet regularly with inclusion specialists. "If there isn't sufficient training of teachers and paraprofessionals, it doesn't work for kids," says Pat Mejia, program director for Support for Families of Children with Disabilities.

Teaching children acceptance. Schools teach inclusive attitudes mostly by example. In addition, a San Francisco organization called Kids Project does school presentations to educate kids about disabilities. "It helps kids to appreciate each other's similarities and differences," says Emily Bittner, program director. "They begin to understand that disabilities are a social, not medical, condition."

Big Challenges, Big Rewards

Inclusive education is, in general, more expensive, says Mc-Knight. It means hiring specially trained paraprofessionals to work with the students and providing training to classroom teachers. Some federal funds are available, but not enough to cover the cost—one reason why inclusion doesn't happen more. In addition, there's rarely enough time in a typical school week for the planning and collaboration necessary to make inclusion work well.

And mainstream classrooms don't work for all students with disabilities. Billy, who has development delays, was fully included in a third-grade classroom with a teacher who lacked training in special needs. Billy was aware that he could not do what his peers were doing and became increasingly frustrated. His behavior got worse. Eventually he was transferred into a special class. With teaching at his own level and an intensive social skills curriculum, he showed great improvement and appeared much happier.

The challenges of inclusion are substantial, but the payoffs come in small day-to-day moments. Tiffany Kendall recalls, for example, the time a fifth-grade student with Down Syndrome, sharing a learning experience with two non-disabled peers, put his arms around their shoulders and said, grinning, "Friends! I love friends!"

"That," says Kendall, "makes it all worthwhile."

Social Inclusion Programs Benefit Students with Disabilities

Louise Fenner

In the following viewpoint, Louise Fenner describes several community-based programs that have increased opportunities for interactions between students with and without intellectual disabilities. She notes that the work of private and nonprofit groups such as Best Buddies, has fostered friendships, broken down social barriers, and decreased isolation for the intellectually disabled through friendship-building activities. By interacting with students without intellectual disabilities, disabled students learn important lessons about themselves, friendship, and social discourse. Louise Fenner is a staff writer for the United States Information Agency (USIA).

For young people who are intellectually disabled, it can be a lonely world. They have few opportunities to play sports, participate in social activities and make friends.

"So often, kids with intellectual disabilities share the hallways, the classrooms, the cafeteria with the other kids in school, but there's no interaction between them. It's almost like an invisible line," says Allison Coles. "It's heartbreaking."

Ending Isolation

Coles directs the Virginia chapter of Best Buddies, a U.S. nonprofit group that fosters friendships between people with and without intellectual disabilities. Best Buddies seeks to end the isolation that plagues many children and adults with Down

Louise Fenner, "Groups Work for Social Inclusion of Intellectually Disabled Kids: Best Buddies, Local Private and Nonprofit Groups Work to End Social Isolation," USInfo .State.gov, October 5, 2007.

syndrome, autism and other intellectual disabilities. There are also many local groups throughout the United States with the same goal.

Best Buddies was started in 1989 by Anthony Kennedy Shriver, whose parents founded Special Olympics nearly 40 years ago.

Best Buddies has about 1400 chapters in colleges and secondary schools in the United States and over 30 other countries, where student volunteers are paired up with "buddies" who have intellectual disabilities. "We ask for the buddy pairs to get together several times a month outside of school and at least once a week in an activity inside the school," Coles told *USINFO.*

"It makes a world of difference to these [special needs] kids," she said. "All of a sudden, students they may have only seen in the cafeteria now recognize them as friends and peers."

Best Buddies also runs an online e-mail friendship program called e-Buddies, and some chapters help people find and retain jobs.

The buddy experience can lead to better social skills, "which can lead to job opportunities," Coles said. She told of a high school graduate named Eric, who has Down syndrome. He attended a Best Buddies event at a local restaurant and "the chef was so taken with him that he was hired as an employee there," she said. "He is thriving."

Life Is Sweet

That chef is one of two dozen in the Washington [D.C.] area who contribute their time at an annual Best Buddies fundraiser called Life Is Sweet. The chefs and their special needs buddies prepare and serve elaborate desserts to some 400 paying guests in a grand ballroom at the Four Seasons Hotel.

Former White House executive pastry chef Roland Mesnier is honorary chair of the event and a huge fan of Best Buddies.

His buddy Brenna Cannon "is absolutely fantastic," Mesnier said. "She steals your heart."

"This is an event I really cherish," he said.

Victoria Paton, coordinator of Life Is Sweet, has been involved with Special Olympics and Best Buddies for many years. She vividly remembers a friend with an autistic son telling her, "The hardest thing about having a child with a mental disability is that they don't have any friends, because it's very difficult for them."

"Best Buddies is really aimed at remedying that," Paton said.

"I think the public is more aware" of the contributions people with intellectual disabilities can make, she added, "and that's where the Shriver family has made a huge difference."

Special-Needs Cheerleading Squads

In addition to Special Olympics and Best Buddies, many community groups and individuals sponsor friendship-building activities. For example, there are some 160 cheerleading squads for young people with special needs and the number is growing, according to the U.S. Allstar Federation (USASF), an international coalition of cheerleading clubs.

In 2006, a group of parents collaborated with Andrea Needle, executive director of the Dream Allstars gym in Gaithersburg, Maryland, to launch a cheerleading squad called Destiny. Because many families face financial hardship from caring for special needs children, Needle provides the coaching, gym space and even the girls' cheerleading uniforms at no cost.

The girls are taught "all the same things" a typical cheerleader learns, but "at a modified pace and less difficult," she said. Some need extra assistance, so several nondisabled cheerleaders volunteer to help each week. In 2006, there were 12 Destiny cheerleaders; this year there are 17 "and we expect more," Needle said.

"The parents tell us all the time what a wonderful thing it has been for their kids," she said. "We've had parents say, 'Before my daughter became part of this team we never had play dates or sleepovers.'"

The Benefits

The girls also learn to focus and follow instructions, improve their physical coordination, and develop confidence. They learn to interact with each other as well as the coach and helpers.

"It has created a community for these kids where they have friends and get to do things other little girls get to do," Needle said. "One father told me that when the girls got their uniforms, his daughter slept in hers all night. She put it on and said 'I look beautiful.'"

She said the volunteers—including her two daughters—also benefit from the experience. "They really have fallen in love with these kids," Needle said.

In cheerleading competitions, "the special needs teams always get a fabulous response from the audience—a standing ovation," Needle said. "It's very moving."

Self-Esteem Is an Exaggerated Need for Students with Disabilities

Richard M. Foxx and Constance E. Roland

In the following selection, Richard M. Foxx and Constance E. Roland discuss the fallacy that self-esteem of disabled students should be a serious consideration in the decision to keep them in a mainstream classroom setting. The authors assert that the concept of self-esteem is a fad and advocates for educational inclusion are using the term as a buzz word. After defining the concept of self-esteem, Foxx and Roland provide an example that supports their supposition that self-esteem is not a measured and quantitative concept with proven worth. Richard Foxx and Constance Roland are professors of psychology at Pennsylvania State University in Harrisburg.

Given the obsession with self-esteem among the general public, regular educators and therapists, it should come as no surprise that it is ardently espoused as being of great importance for individuals with developmental disabilities. This is especially true of those advocating for educational inclusion because assessment of one's inclusionary status is thought to determine one's self-esteem. Yet, a close examination of self-esteem reveals that it easily meets the definition of a fad, as there is little or no empirical evidence that it is of any real value to those having or lacking it. Self-esteem also has been labeled as a myth and a major contributor to overindulgent childrearing practices.

We begin by looking at why the general public and the psychological/educational community view self-esteem as im-

Richard M. Foxx and Constance E. Roland, "The Self-Esteem Fallacy," *Controversial Therapies for Developmental Disabilities*, Mahwah, NJ: Lawrence Erlbaum Associates Publishers, 2005, pp. 101–110. Copyright © 2005 by Lawrence Erlbaum Associates, Inc. All rights reserved. Reproduced by permission.

portant. We next examine why its importance is highly questionable. The chapter concludes with a case from a due process hearing that illustrates how those touting inclusion in the education of individuals with developmental disabilities and autism have linked it to increases in the self-esteem of special and regular education students that make no educational sense.

A Definition of Self-Esteem

The concept of self-esteem is grounded in the theories of self-concept. As such, self-esteem is a self-evaluation of competency ratios and opinions of significant others that results in either a positive or negative evaluation of one's worthiness. [Psychologist] William James first discussed self-esteem as part of his theory of self-concept. His definition of *social self* (the importance of the evaluations of others) is closer to what we currently regard as self-esteem than what he described as self-esteem. [Psychologist and professor] J.D. Brown has argued that self-esteem is grounded in affective, rather than cognitive, processes and that feelings are most important to individuals. Thus, individuals do not just think positive or negative thoughts about themselves, they feel good or bad about themselves.

When individuals seek inclusion in a group or when their inclusionary status within a group is threatened, they are motivated to behave in ways that will maintain their inclusion or increase the potential for inclusion. This motivation could be positive, for example, attending and participating in math club and wearing a pocket protector in order to be accepted as a math whiz, or negative, for example, defacing a school building in order to be accepted as a gang member. In effect, in their effort to increase self-esteem, individuals can behave without serious thought as to positive or negative consequences of their actions.

Self-esteem is regarded as a key to understanding normal, abnormal, and optimal behavior. Many parents and caregivers believe that if their children or charges do not feel good about themselves, that is, have high self-esteem, they will be at risk for any number of emotional and psychological problems. Higher levels of self-esteem are said to be associated with high ego functioning, personal adjustment, internal control, favorable therapy outcomes, positive adjustment to old age, and autonomy. A lack of self-esteem is suggested to be related to negative outcomes, including some mental disorders such as depression and suicide and social problems such as substance abuse, teen pregnancies, school dropout rates, and delinquency.

Many therapists have accepted the notion that if "we could only enhance their self-esteem, then everything would be so much better." Parallel with the belief that low self-esteem causes emotional distress and dysfunctional behavior is the belief that high self-esteem is related to optimal mental health. "Its general importance to a full spectrum of effective human behaviors remains virtually uncontested." N. Branden, one of the leading popularizers of self-esteem, stated that he could not think of a single psychological problem that was not traceable to low self-esteem. He also believed that as someone's self-esteem increased, there was an increased likelihood of that person treating others with respect, kindness, and generosity. A.M. Mecca ... [and others] identified self-esteem as a causal factor in personal and social responsibility. . . .

Self-Esteem and Education

Self-esteem appears to be an important concern of advocates for educational inclusion. J.W. Jacobson reported that his survey of ERIC [Education Resources Information Center] from 1990 to 2000 revealed 85 references to the key terms *inclusion and self-esteem* but only 45 to *mental retardation* and *self-esteem*. Yet, L.G. Daniel and D.A. King suggested that inclusive groupings are associated with greater instances of behavior problems, student gains in only one instructional area, and lowered levels of self-esteem. The following case supports their contention as well as a number of the points made in J.M. Kauffman and D.P. Hallahan.

Several years ago one of the authors was asked by a school district to evaluate whether or not a 10-year-old boy's educational needs were being met. The school district had requested an Individual with Disabilities Education Act (IDEA) hearing before a special education officer because it contended that it could not provide FAPE (a free and appropriate public education) to the boy by keeping him in a regular classroom as his parents and their inclusion expert insisted. Rather, the district sought to place the boy in a resource setting for several hours per day. The author's evaluation included a review of voluminous records; the inclusion expert's reports over the years; interviews with the boy's teachers, aide, and parents, the school principal, the school district's special education director, and attorney; and direct observations of the boy in all of his school settings. After filing the report, the author would be serving as the school's expert witness at the hearing.

The boy was nonverbal, not toilet trained, aggressive, and took food from others in the cafeteria. In kindergarten through second grade, he was included in regular education classes with support from a one-to-one aide in the classroom and received one hour per day of pull-out services from a special education teacher. In Grades 3 and 4, he continued to be included in regular education classes and received one-to-one support but his pull-out services were terminated.

By Grade 5, the school district requested the IDEA hearing because it contended that it could not provide FAPE to the boy in the regular classroom but could do so in a resource setting. The district noted that over the prior 2 years, it had been very difficult to either schedule an ARD (Areas of Disagreement) meeting with the parents, finish a meeting, or

127

participate in a meeting that was not highly contentious. Perhaps not surprisingly, one item from a list of points of agreement between the school and parents was that the boy's diaper would be checked each hour and changed if appropriate.

The battle lines were clearly drawn. The school district, with the author serving as an expert, sought to meet the boy's educational needs via a plan that addressed his needs and level of functioning. The parents, local advocacy group and its attorneys, and an inclusion expert sought to maintain the status quo wherein the boy remained included throughout most of the school day. One of their bedrock issues was that the boy's "self-esteem" as well as that of his regular education classmates would and had been positively affected by the inclusion experience.

To frame the issues, we shall discuss the reports and classroom observations of the inclusion expert, an independent autism specialist's report and the author.

Inclusion Expert's Reports

The expert's initial inclusion plan and observations were written when the boy was in third grade. It had been followed for 2 years and was a major part of the expert's testimony. A second report was written for the hearing. Both reports had all of the requisite inclusion concepts, buzzwords, and underlying ideology.

Inclusion Plan:

Inclusion Builds Self-Esteem and Acceptance. The expert indicated that inclusion in regular classroom activities would raise the boy's self-esteem by heightening his feelings of acceptance by classmates and the other students in the school. The regular education teacher was urged to take ownership of the boy in order to have him perceived as a legitimate member of the class. By taking ownership, the teacher would prevent the boy from being "velcroed to his aide and this, in turn, would enhance his positive perception of himself." The students would perceive the boy as a classmate and one of them rather than as a visitor or outsider.

Inclusion Must Be Maintained at All Costs to Prevent a Loss of Self-Esteem. The expert strongly felt that once the boy was accepted by the other students, they would have greater tolerance for the problem behaviors that he was known to display. Furthermore, it was important to his self-esteem that when he had a behavior episode that he remain in the classroom unless it became "*totally impossible to conduct classroom activities or for the other students to attend to their work*" (italics added).

The More Opportunities for Inclusion, the More Appropriate the Service Delivery and the Greater Opportunity to Raise Self-Esteem. The expert equated the appropriateness of service delivery with the extent and number of opportunities available to the boy to participate in the regular curriculum. For example, it was suggested that during spelling exercises, the boy have the opportunity to select the word others were to spell. Picking the word for his classmates was said to be a reward and a way of keeping him on task. Additionally, it would build his self-esteem.

Inclusion Is Learner Centered and Builds Self-Esteem. The report indicated that it was important to make the curriculum inclusive for all students and that doing so offered benefits in regards to self-esteem. Inclusive methods were reported to be much more learner centered than traditional methods. Being learner centered, these methods were uniquely designed to help the student have a positive experience in school. They also were regarded as more creative than traditional methods.

Classroom Observations:

The inclusion expert's observations in the classroom revealed the boy's actions did not suggest that his self-esteem was being enhanced by his inclusion experience.

The boy was described as sometimes sitting with other students but not participating in their activities. He appeared distracted and inattentive when other children were asked to interact with him. He seemed bored since he acted tired, closed his eyes and wanted to rest frequently. On some occasions he became quite agitated such as when the lights were turned out or when he attempted to grab food in the cafeteria. . . .

The Self-Esteem Fallacy

The author's report contained a number of sharply worded conclusions. One concerned the inclusion expert's assertion that the boy's self-esteem would be raised in a regular classroom. The author pointed out that the expert offered no way of measuring self-esteem or building it other than blind faith. Furthermore, being pulled from a regular class is no more embarrassing or stigmatizing than receiving help in the classroom. . . .

The report concluded that the dispute between the school district and the boy's parents reflected the division in special education between process (placement with same-aged peers to enhance, among other things, self-esteem) versus outcome (the boy learning) and between social philosophy (inclusion at all costs) versus scholarly research (sound educational practices appropriately developed for an individual).

The due process hearing lasted several days and included testimony by the author, inclusion expert, regular and special education teachers, the school district's special education director, and the boy's parents. The hearing officer ultimately agreed with the school district and concluded that the school district could not continue to provide FAPE to the boy unless he received instruction in a resource setting for several hours per day. The hearing officer did not address whether or not the boy's self-esteem would be affected as a result of the decision.

An Appropriate Education Should Be Guaranteed for All, Despite Funding Issues

Greg Cruey

In the following viewpoint, Greg Cruey supports the funding of public special-education programs that educate children with disabilities. Cruey asserts that the disabled have a basic human right to a good education, and reduced funding violates their rights. He argues that violating a disabled child's right to a free and appropriate education is illegal and cannot be overlooked in favor of budgeting. Greg Cruey is an educator and journalist who specializes in teaching children with disabilities.

One of the more confusing discussions in special education circles in the U.S. is the one over funding the provision of services to students with disabilities.

While we tend to think in terms of legislation when we consider the rights of special education students, the truth is that laws have consistently been passed by Congress primarily to *catch up* to what the courts have ruled *must* happen. Students with disabilities in America have a right to a free, appropriate public education (a FAPE), *not* because Congress made it law, but because the courts have said so—first in 1971 in the case *Pennsylvania ARC v. the Commonwealth of Pennsylvania*, and again the next year in *Mills v. the Board of Education*. The Education for All Handicapped Children Act (EAHCA, later to become the Individuals with Disabilities Education Act, or IDEA) was an attempt in 1975 to bring order and legal organization to the rights the courts had already recognized.

Greg Cruey, "Full Funding & Rights," Suite101.com, July 7, 2006. Reproduced by permission of the author.

Consider this:

- When the U.S. Supreme Court ruled in 1954 in *Brown v. Board of Education [of Topeka, Kansas]* that city and county school systems all across America would have to integrate their schools, not a penny in funding for the task was attached to the ruling.

- In 1972, when the Patsy T. Mink Equal Opportunity in Education Act (eventually to become known as Title IX) was passed requiring some level of parity in funding for sports for men and women, no funding was committed to that.

- When the Rehabilitation Act (including section 504, which prohibits discrimination against people with disabilities) was passed in 1973, not a cent was appropriated to help local government agencies comply with the new law's requirements.

- In 1990 the Americans with Disabilities Act was made law and extended still more civil rights protections to the disabled without a single thin dime of funding.

Rights Do Not Require Special Funding

Rights are rights. And one of the most profound and fundamental values of American society is the idea that *money* can't buy you your rights. Neither can your lack of money cost you your rights.

So when Congress began, as part of the debate over passing EAHCA, to try and estimate the *cost* of educating students with disabilities in the public schools, the waters were muddied and clarity of thought on the topic has often been reduced as a result. The idea developed in many state and local educational agencies that the right of a severely retarded child, or of a blind and deaf girl, or of a Down syndrome boy to a

FAPE was somehow contingent upon the degree to which federal funding could be used to secure that child's right.

A monetary value was placed on a basic right in American society.

It would be nice if the federal government thought that the value of educating the disabled was worth more. It would be nice, for that matter, if the federal government thought that education in general was worth a greater investment. I'd be for that—for money to lower the student-teacher ratio in American schools and to raises [of] teacher pay so that salaries reflect the level or training and professionalism required to do the job. Instead the current [George W. Bush] administration's long-term goal seems to be the privatization of education in America and the dismantling of Great Society programs [established under President Lyndon Johnson in the 1960s] like Title I [enacted to improve the academic achievement of the disadvantaged].

The truth is that regardless of the federal government's willingness (or unwillingness) to *fund* special education in individual states from Washington's coffers, kids with autism or dyslexia, with emotional disturbances or traumatic brain injury have an *unmitigated right* to an education. A *free* education. An *appropriate* education. That's not to say that a disabled child has a right to the *best* available education; but they do have a right to an appropriate one.

The funding issue is simple, really. When a school system says that it can't provide that kind of education because, well, it can't afford to, it is offering to violate that child's civil rights. And it bears liability for that regardless of federal funding priorities in the current fiscal year.

Funding for Special Education Is Excessive

Robert Worth

In the following selection, journalist Robert Worth addresses the failings of the Individuals with Disabilities Education Act that mandated the special-education system. Worth feels that a disproportionate amount of money is spent on special education while slighting other programs, including aid for poor children. Programs for conventional students also are underfunded, argues Worth, due to the excessive amount of money needed to maintain what he labels the special-education bureaucracy. On the whole, Worth asserts, the special-education system is an expensive, wasteful failure.

If you've ever wondered what the words "special education" mean, consider Saundra Lemons. A tall, gangly 19 year-old senior in a Washington D.C. public high school, she is quiet and attentive. Like the vast majority of children in special ed [education], she's not blind or deaf or confined to a wheelchair; instead, she has had trouble learning to read. If dollars were education, Saundra would be in fine shape. D.C. pours almost a third of its total education budget into the 10 percent of its students who are special ed. In theory—or rather, in wealthy school districts—this money buys kids like Saundra all kinds of assistance: special tutoring sessions, a modified curriculum, specially trained therapists and consultants, even untimed tests.

But Saundra wasn't born in a wealthy suburb. So when she started having trouble in first grade, she was placed—like many kids in D.C.—into a dead-end classroom where she

Robert Worth, "The Scandal of Special Ed," *Washington Monthly*, vol. 31, no. 6, 1999. Copyright © 1999 by Washington Monthly Publishing, LLC, 733 15th St. NW, Suite 520, Washington DC 20005, (202) 393-5155, www.washingtonmonthly.com. Reproduced by permission.

learned nothing. In her case, it was a class for the mentally retarded. It took six years for a teacher to notice that Saundra wasn't retarded at all. Now she's catching up, but probably not fast enough to attend college next year. "You can never make up for that lost time," says one social worker who has helped Saundra.

Spending Too Much Money in a Biased Manner

Twenty five years after the passage of the nation's special ed law, the Individuals with Disabilites Education Act (IDEA), the real scandal is not simply that we spend too much to educate handicapped kids. It's the inequity in the way the law is applied. At an estimated $35 billion a year, special education is like a huge regressive tax—helpful to those wealthy enough to take advantage of it, and often harmful to those who are not.

Furthermore, poor children like Saundra who get shunted into dead-end classrooms aren't the only victims. In order to pay for special ed's enormous, ineffectual bureaucracy and skyrocketing enrollments, school districts are being forced to cheat their conventional students. Unlike general education, special ed is a federal mandate: School districts can be sued (and routinely are) for not providing every service parents think is appropriate for their disabled kids. It's also massively underfunded. When IDEA was passed in 1975, the feds offered to pay up to 40 percent of the costs. They've averaged less than 10 percent ever since, and states don't make up the difference. This is not the kind of program you can fund with bakesales. One southern California district has seen its special ed layouts grow from $3 million to almost $11 million in just the past three years. School districts face a painful choice: raise local property taxes or cut back on students. "We are cannibalizing our regular education budget," says Joe Quick, an administrator in the Wisconsin public school system. "For the first time since 1975, teachers are saying 'why are those kids here?' It's really starting to drive a wedge between regular ed and special ed."

Republicans in Congress have pounced on this issue, declaring [President Bill] Clinton a hypocrite for announcing new school initiatives without promising to increase special education funding first. "What President Clinton isn't saying about his new budget is how he has decided to trim special education funding," declared Rep. Bill Goodling (R-Pa.), a former teacher and superintendent and chair of the House Education and the Workforce Committee, in March [1999]. "The president decided not to provide funding for our most vulnerable children," added Senate Majority Leader Trent Lott. The irony here is delicious: The [Democratic] party that tried to abolish the Department of Education and slash the federal role in education has now become a cheerleader for the most regulated and costly federal program under the sun.

Democrats counter that their plan to hire 100,000 new teachers will reduce the need for referrals to special ed in the first place. But neither party has even tried to reform special ed's mountainous bureaucracy and skewed incentives. It's not hard to see why. "If you criticize [IDEA] you will be publicly villified as anti-handicap," says James Fleming, superintendent of the Capistrano Unified school district, near Los Angeles. "But what is happening now will absolutely destroy public education before the next decade is out."

Good Intentions

There's no question that the special ed law served a crying need. Before Congress passed it in 1975, an estimated one million handicapped kids were not getting any education at all, and vastly disporportionate numbers of black children were being warehoused under the rubric "educably mentally retarded." The new law's intention was to remedy these conditions by mandating "specially designed instruction" for each child and "related services to meet his unique needs," including transportation, physical therapy, speech therapy, psychological counseling, occupational therapy, social work and services, and virtually anything else a child might conceivably need. To ensure that no one was left out, Congress mandated that each handicapped child receive an Individualized Education Plan from a multi-disciplinary team, which would specify long- and short-term goals, and describe required services and special equipment. Furthermore, handicapped children had to be taught in the "least restrictive environment."

Benefits of IDEA

IDEA has achieved some of its main goals. Far fewer handicapped children sit at home staring at the walls, and the number attending college has more than tripled since 1978. According to the Department of Education, 62 percent of people with disabilities age 16 to 24 were employed in 1994, compared with 31 percent in the 16 to 64 age range—which suggests that far more are entering the workplace than ever before.

At first, accommodating the handicapped didn't seem like such a big job; total costs were about $1 billion in 1977. Yet little by little, Congress has added new categories to the original list of 13 disabling conditions. Children age three to five are now included, as are those with autism and traumatic brain injuries—both categories that require intensive supervision and therapy. In March [1999], the Supreme Court ruled that an Iowa school district must pay for full-time nursing care for a high school sophomore named Garret Frey who is paralyzed from the neck down. Meanwhile the most porous special ed category, "learning disabilities," exploded as parents realized it could be made to include virtually any child who isn't living up to his potential. "It's just like a nightmare," says April Port, special ed director for Marin County, Calif. "They keep opening the barn door wider and wider, and the burden is always on the school." Currently, special ed costs the nation about $35 billion, with some estimates running closer to $60 billion.

Family-Specific Demands

In almost any individual case, it's hard not to sympathize with the family. Garret Frey is a likeable, smart kid, who has no trouble keeping up with his peers academically. For all we know, he could become a great scientist like the wheelchair-bound Stephen Hawking, the theorist of space-time. But he won't be able to do so unless someone pays for his medical supervision. Handicapped kids often struggle heroically to get by in school, and it's no wonder their parents feel entitled to extra help. One father told me in a voice choking with rage about how he had gone to school to confront a teacher who had taunted and bullied his boy, who has severe learning disabilities. "You hear about some parents demanding horseback riding lessons for their autistic kids, and it sounds ludicrous," another parent told me. "But when you see what they're going through, believe me, you want to do anything you can if there's any chance it would help."

The trouble is that the law pits the single interest of every disabled child against the broader interest of the school and arms his parents with a legal right to a "free and appropriate public education" in "least restrictive environment." Needless to say, the vagueness of these words is a recipe for litigation. A whole cottage industry of lawyers and advocates has grown up to help parents get what they want out of the school system. Furthermore, school districts must pay parents' court fees if they lose. Overburdened, underfunded, and without the expert legal advice parents can draw on, schools tend to give in rather than face a case that could bankrupt them. "Districts will provide services they don't think are appropriate because they can't afford to go to court," says April Port. One southern California school district pays for a severely brain-damaged boy to attend a specialized school in Massachusetts, and to fly his parents and sister out for regular visits, at an annual cost of roughly $254,000. The superintendent only balked when the family demanded extra visits for the boy's sister.

Parents of severely disabled kids also regularly try to shoe-horn them into mainstream classes, even when it would do little good for the child and plenty of harm to the rest of the class. It's true that for years schools were too quick to put seriously handicapped kids into classes of their own, where they often learned little and got no experience interacting with ordinary people. But special ed teachers tend to agree that the pendulum has now swung too far in the other direction. "It's hard for parents to give up the dream that their kid is normal," says April Port. The 1997 amendments to the IDEA strengthen the parents' hands: Teachers must prove that a child would be better off in separate classes before they move them, and that can be very hard to do. "Often you'll have a kid with a 40 or 50 IQ, at a pre-kindergarten level, with very little language," says one California elementary school teacher. "The kid is all over the place, and the teacher has no idea what to do." In response, many districts are paying for aides—babysitters, really—to sit with the student all day long. "Mainstreaming is creating a huge financial burden," says Port.

Definition of Disability is Expanding

Still, if special ed were merely a matter of accommodating physically disabled kids like Garret Frey, it would be a relatively straightforward affair. Unfortunately, the special ed law has inflated the meaning of "disability," encouraging wealthier families to capitalize on their weaknesses at the expense of their peers. "We are talking about kids who get tired," says Superintendent James Fleming of Capistrano Unified. "We are talking about people thinking any problem their kid has is a handicap." At worst, the handicap designation—designed to protect kids from discrimination—can become a protection against any sort of discipline. "We found one kid with enough pot on him to be selling," says Fleming. "We suspended him. Then the parents were contacted by an advocate who said 'all you have to say is that you're handicapped.' Sure enough, the kid was back in school the next day. The kids he sold to were expelled." The 1997 amendments to IDEA gave schools a little more latitude in disciplining violent special ed kids, but the problem remains.

Meanwhile, the largest area of disability inflation, known as "specific learning disabilities," remains unaddressed. Learning disabilities, or LDs, account for over 51 percent of all children in special ed, and the numbers are growing at astounding speed. Technically, the 1975 law defines LD as "a disorder in one or more of the basic psychological processes involved in understanding or in using language, spoken or written, which disorder may manifest itself in imperfect ability to listen, think, speak, read, write, spell, or do mathematical calculations." Lest this be an open invitation to anyone who has trouble with their homework, the regulations stipulate that a diagnostic team shall identify as LD those students who show a "severe discrepancy" between their achievement in one or more subject areas and their intelligence, usually as measured by an IQ test.

Difficulties Defining Disability

Yet even with this diagnostic testing, LD is a notoriously plastic category. There are 50 state definitions in addition to the federal one, and the methods used to determine intelligence vary wildly. More than 80 percent of all school children in the United States could qualify as learning-disabled under one definition or another, according to University of Minnesota researcher James Ysseldyke. Even if LDs do exist as a legitimate category, it is not a foregone conclusion that learning-disabled children should receive more help than garden variety poor readers. Why should a kid with a genius IQ but only above-average reading skills get extra help, while his average-scoring peers get none—no matter what obstacles they've overcome? It seems especially unfair that the rules should specifically exclude kids whose learning problems derive from "environmental, cultural, or economic disadvantage."

LD advocates respond by citing voluminous studies purporting to demonstrate that LDs are real, and that they respond to treatment. But the scientific status of LDs is still cloudy at best, and it's not clear that LD students respond any better than their undiagnosed peers. Indeed, "[T]here is considerable evidence that non-LD pupils would benefit from higher levels of educational inputs, and even stronger evidence that as a group, if not in each individual case, those diagnosed with LDs have been remarkably unresponsive to the costly special education that has been provided to them," write Mark Kelman and Gillian Lester in their 1998 book, *Jumping the Queue: An Inquiry into the Legal Treatment of Students with Learning Disabilities.* "There is very scant evidence that dyslexics, for instance, benefit more from the interventions of reading specialists than do garden variety poor readers."

Furthermore, the LD diagnosis is often little more than an expression of class bias. As Kelman and Lester write, "a student is viewed as LD when the observer finds it surprising that he or she is performing poorly." These expectations, of course, are likely to be informed by the parents' social status. Learning disabilities grew out of a grassroots movement by middle-class parents in the 1950s and '60s who wanted a label—and extra help—for what they saw as their "underachieving" children. That's not to say that some bright kids don't suffer from dyslexia and other serious reading problems. But there's little doubt that the meaning of the LD diagnosis depends, in large measure, on who your parents are.

Consider Michael, a slender, sandy-haired fourth grader in a public school in Marin, one of California's wealthiest counties. Michael's teacher says he has an IQ in the high 120s, but he's about two years behind his classmates in reading. His parents are both wealthy professionals who don't have much time to spend with him—which may account for his reading problems. But his teachers didn't want lawsuits, so they wrote an education plan that includes a modified curriculum with separate tests, special reading sessions in a "resource" room, a buddy to read with, and books on tape to keep him on track. If his problems persist, his parents will see to it that he gets any other accommodations the school can offer, including untimed tests, and eventually, an untimed SAT [Scholastic Assessment Test], to increase his chances of going to Stanford [University] like Mom and Dad did. "We get a lot of referrals junior year," says another teacher in Michael's school. "Parents want to cut their kid a break. And it's starting a lot earlier." The words LD, she adds, no longer have any tainting stigma. Yale psychologist Robert J. Sternberg, who has spent years preparing a book on LDs, agrees. "That's the funny thing—before, no one would want that label. Now it's almost a cachet."

Despite the fact that LD isn't meant to apply to kids whose problems derive from poverty, teachers in poorer schools routinely bend the rules in order to get more attention for kids who are failing. Crowded and decaying inner-city classrooms are a handicap in their own right, and poverty itself can cut deeply into a child's learning. According to the Children's Defense Fund, middle-class children starting first grade have been exposed to 1,000 to 1,700 hours of one-on-one reading, while their low-income counterparts have been exposed to only 25 hours. It's little wonder that so many of these kids get referred to special ed.

But these efforts often backfire when the students end up in dead-end classrooms where they'll be even less likely to learn. "You need to look at who gets the benefits of being diagnosed LD and who gets the bad side," says Mark Kelman. Tony, an African-American boy from northeast Washington,

D.C., is fairly typical. He was diagnosed with learning disabilities a few years ago at roughly the same age as Michael. Like many kids in large urban school systems, he didn't get any help at all, and began falling further behind. Unhappy with his failures, he began "acting out" in class, whereupon he was reassessed and classified "emotionally disturbed" and put into separate classes. There he was taught nothing and his behavior got worse, because many of his genuinely disturbed classmates picked fights with him. By the sixth grade he barely knew the alphabet. Yet Tony is neither stupid nor disturbed. A public interest lawyer managed to work a minor miracle, getting him assessed and transferred to a private school, where he has thrived. "If he'd had the appropriate intervention in third or fourth grade," says the lawyer, "who knows where he'd be now."

According to researchers who have studied trends in the treatment of LD across the country, these patterns apply nationwide. Kelman and Lester argue that the current system "continues to permit relatively privileged white pupils to capture high-cost or non-stigmatic in-class resources that others with similar educational deficits cannot obtain while, at the same time, allowing disproportionate numbers of African-American and poor pupils to be shunted into self-contained classes."

A Flawed System

Why does special ed serve the poor so badly? Part of the answer has to do with its massive, ineffectual, and self-perpetuating bureaucracy. Beneath the federal Office of Special Education Programs, which does research and audits states and school districts, there is a state office, and a localized Special Education Local Plan Area office, and a school district office. This is all on top of whatever counselors, psychologists, therapists, and "educational evaluators" a given school may have working for it. And in some individual states and cities, the situation is even worse. New York City, for instance, has its own separate bureaucracy, jokingly called the "Board of Special Ed," thanks to consent decree that grew out of a lawsuit by advocates for special ed students in 1979.

Given this focus on legal liability and procedure, it's little wonder that teaching takes a back seat to paper-pushing. "[Special ed teachers] complain they're spending 50 to 60 percent of their time filling out forms," says Kim Reid, a professor at Columbia Teachers' College. This constant bureaucratic drain makes it that much harder to recruit talented young people. It's bad enough dealing with disabled or disturbed children and their grieving, angry parents all day. The job is so stressful that the average shelf life of special ed teachers is three years, says Reid. The Department of Education website, which proudly displays the voluminous 1997 amendments to the IDEA, notes tersely a "'chronic' shortage of special education teachers who are fully certified in their positions."

Problems with Special Education

The burden of this teacher crisis, and the top-heavy bureaucracy that fuels it, falls disproportionately on the poor. Wealthier parents, after all, can use the law to force schools to accommodate them or place their child in a private school. In Washington, D.C., such private placements account for over a third of the district's entire $167 million special ed budget, even though less than one-sixth of the district's special ed students attend private school. (The special ed budget itself comprises almost a third of the entire school budget, even though only one-tenth of the district's students are in special ed.)

What is left over for the students whose parents lack the money or know-how to work the system to their advantage? Precious little. Despite all those bureaucrats hired to evaluate and place students, more than 250 students in D.C. haven't received an initial evaluation, and almost 2,200 are overdue for their second evaluation. Many of these kids are like Saundra

Lemons, languishing in inappropriate classes until an "evaluator" notices them. Often it's far too late by that time, since the crucial learning years are the earliest, and catching up is far more difficult when children are older. And being evaluated doesn't always help. "Often the kid ends up in a class with 20 kids, all with different disabilities, and a teacher who's trained in one of those," says Nancy Opalack, a D.C. social worker. "No one learns anything." Teachers in the district estimate that half the kids in special ed drop out by 10th grade.

Gross Inequities

Yet anyone who's spent time in an inner-city classroom can tell you that the challenges the average poor kid faces are often hard to distinguish from those you'll find in special ed. This may be the greatest absurdity of the special ed law: It fails to acknowledge "environmental, cultural, or economic disadvantage" as disabling conditions. Why should a child with a broken back be guaranteed round-the clock, state-of-the-art medical care, no matter what the cost, while the millions of kids whose difficulties stem from poverty and neglect are left to hope that their teachers will break the rules so they can get some extra help? Should we really be spending $10 billion (at least) a year on "learning disabilites" when we still don't adequately fund Head Start and Title I, the federal programs that were designed to help poor children catch up with their wealthier peers?

If the goal of public education is to give everyone a roughly equal start by the time they reach adulthood, it simply doesn't make sense to privilege obstacles that can be given a medical diagnosis over those that derive from poverty—which may be the greatest handicapping condition of all. The fact that the special ed bureaucracy often prevents poor kids from getting the help they need, by making them wait until they've been properly evaluated, only adds insult to injury.

Reforming IDEA is no easy task. Any politician who touches it runs the risk of being branded a cold-hearted enemy of kids in wheelchairs. But before we start pouring billions more into the program, Congress should ask whether it's really serving the goal of equal opportunity for all. And if special ed has become a kind of band-aid for schools that lack money to teach their kids adequately, or for kids whose parents never prepared them in the first place, then perhaps it's time to address those problems head-on. Kids like Garret Frey deserve a shot at success—but not at the expense of kids like Saundra Lemons.

The Impact of
Technological Advances
on the Disabled

Chapter Preface

In 1951 Dr. Howard Rusk returned from duty in World War II, where he worked with injured soldiers, and opened the Institute of Rehabilitation Medicine at New York University Medical Center. At the rehabilitation center, Rusk applied his military training to civilian life as he and his staff developed technology to assist individuals with severe disabilities deal with daily life situations. This application of technology was celebrated by the disabled community without further debate. Subsequent technological advances related to disabilities, however, have not always been considered helpful or benign.

Technological advances in medicine, computers, and electronics have provided ways to circumnavigate or functionally eliminate disability. While some individuals with disabilities fully accept technological advances, others view them with suspicion and concern. One such example is the deaf community's reaction to the cochlear implant, a device that consists of an external microphone and speech processor attached to electrodes implanted in the hollow tube of the inner ear. Cochlear implants allow individuals with some types of hearing loss to recognize sounds. Opponents of cochlear implants in the deaf community consider the inability to hear to be a difference in human experience rather than a disability. The idea that a surgical implant could provide a version of hearing and return hearing-impaired individuals to the general population and away from the deaf community is considered a threat. The implants are also viewed as a devaluation of deaf culture, and individuals who choose to get the implants are seen as pulling away from deaf culture.

Another technological advancement that is viewed as a threat by some disability advocates is prenatal and genetic testing that is able to detect potential abnormalities prior to birth. Opponents of the practice believe prenatal and genetic testing is an attempt to eradicate disabled individuals and that it also diminishes the worth of those already born. Inherent in this debate is the battle of parental rights versus the rights of the disabled child before and after birth, especially concerning abortion and the sterilization of the severely disabled.

In the following selections, the authors address these and other issues faced by the disabled in a world filled with new, often controversial, technology. The viewpoints offer differing perspectives on the impact that new technologies may have on people with disabilities.

Cochlear Implants Increase Full Participation in Life for the Deaf

Arlene Romoff

In the following viewpoint, author and cochlear implant recipient Arlene Romoff discusses the benefits of cochlear implant hearing devices. Romoff relates her decision to take advantage of the technological advances that produced the cochlear implants. She does not see a conflict in advocating and participating in the deaf community and being able to hear through the use of technology.

Audiology Online: Hi Arlene. Thanks for your time today. I'd like to start by asking you a little about your hearing and your hearing loss. Did you have normal hearing as a child?

Arlene Romoff: Yes. I had normal hearing until my late teen years, and then it started to decline gradually. I got my first hearing aid at age 23 and over the next 20 or so years it gradually declined to the profound level.

Were your physicians able to determine the cause of the hearing loss?

No, they could never determine a particular cause. I suspect it's some sort of allergic situation, but it was nothing I could ever prove or control. So I watched my hearing continue to deteriorate and when my hearing got to the point where hearing aids could no longer function effectively for me, I became a heavy user of assistive listening devices—in particular an auxiliary microphone plugged directly into my hearing aid. After a while, even that no longer worked for me, and that's when I knew I needed a cochlear implant. I had

Arlene Romoff, "Interview with Arlene Romoff, Author and Cochlear Implant Recipient," *Audiology Online*, March 24, 2003. www.audiologyonline.com. Reprinted with permission.

been following the progress of research with cochlear implants so I had a pretty good idea of what was available and what to expect.

Having a Cochlear Implant

What year did you get your cochlear implant?

1997. I just had my fifth anniversary—I can't believe it's been that long already. It's made such a difference in my life—the improvement in my communication ability has really been amazing.

Yes. It really is. One thing I like to remind readers of is that this is a phone interview. I'm in Texas and you're in New Jersey and obviously you're understanding me quite well, even though I'm using a speaker phone!

Right. I'm using the telephone just listening through the microphone of the implant.

That's pretty amazing.

It always amazes people when I use the phone—but it usually takes a little while before it dawns on them that they're speaking with a totally deaf person. It's kind of mind boggling. Nonetheless, I never take my hearing for granted—not one moment of the day do I take it for granted.

What did you expect when you got your implant and what's been the most surprising thing about it?

Well, as I wrote in my book [*Hear Again*], I just couldn't believe that there could really be a device that would actually allow me to hear again. I found the reality of that to be the most startling revelation of all. I had been going deaf for almost 30 years and with almost no hearing left, I simply couldn't imagine that I would ever be able to hear again. I was afraid that I wouldn't even remember how to hear again. It seemed like an impossible dream.

You've taken a unique approach in writing your book. It's more like a day-by-day diary, isn't it?

Yes, it's a chronicle of my first year with my cochlear implant—a day-by-day account of what it was like to return to a world of sound. It didn't start out being a book. As you can imagine in 1997, not that many people had cochlear implants. People may have heard about them, but they didn't really know how far the technology had come—and how well people could hear with them. I'm very active in advocacy for deaf and hard of hearing people and have been active since before the ADA [Americans with Disabilities Act]. So I have many friends and colleagues, and many of them are either hearing impaired or are hearing professionals, and they were interested in following my progress with my cochlear implant.

The first day I was hooked up, I sent an email to about 75 people plus an Internet bulletin board, and just told them what it was like, and I got a few responses back encouraging me to tell them more. So I sent an email about my experiences on the second day, and even more people responded. They wanted to know more. On the fourth day, a deluge of emails came in. They were just pleading with me to keep writing—and since these included professionals, as well as people considering getting a cochlear implant themselves, I continued writing my daily reports. They found it fascinating. Actually, my advocacy efforts have always been geared to making something good come from my hearing loss, so being able to help people by reporting my experiences and insights fit me quite nicely. I got wonderful feedback from people who read my daily messages, and it became clear there was a great need for this. I kept writing for a year—and these emails became the basis of the book.

So the whole thing wasn't actually planned, it just evolved?

Yes. I sort of stepped into this gradually. After three months, people were encouraging me to have this material published, but I knew that one year would give a more accurate account of the cochlear implant experience.

Let's talk a little bit about how people can get a copy of this book if they want to learn about your one-on-one personal experience with cochlear implants?

The title is *Hear Again* with the subtitle of *Back to Life with a Cochlear Impact*. It was published initially by The League for the Hard of Hearing Publications, the publications division of the League. It has since been picked up by a mainstream publisher and distributor, Sterling Publishing Co., Inc., in New York. . . .

Discussions About Cochlear Implants

The response has been far beyond my expectations! What I found was that even among people who themselves were cochlear implant candidates, they had no idea that the technology had reached the point where people could function so well with a cochlear implant. Some people tracked me down to tell me the impact the book has had on their lives. It's really been very rewarding. When somebody tells you you saved my life, you remember that. When somebody tells you your book is my Bible, or, I wouldn't have sought a cochlear implant if I hadn't read your book, it's a very humbling experience. Professionals have also found it useful, and have endorsed it and recommended it to their colleagues and patients. And parents have thanked me for writing it because it gives them a glimpse at what their children are experiencing.

Yes. I'm sure that must be a very satisfying experience for you. What is your favorite part of the book, or—what's the one thing you hope everybody reads?

That's a tough question because it's chock full of favorites! The book compares and contrasts what life was like before and after getting my cochlear implant—being able to hear versus not being able to hear. So the one episode that somehow encapsulates that best was the one in an elevator where somebody asked me a question. With my cochlear implant, I could chat casually with them—whereas before, I would have preferred to be invisible. The elevator incident cuts to the core of how hearing loss impacts the individual. It's about being so cut off from other people that you don't even want them to talk to you, and that event touches the very essence of the pain and the anguish of hearing loss that so few people realize—unless they've experienced it.

I've had a lot of feedback from people with hearing loss—they all seem to have their favorite episodes. And they've even told me they wished their hearing professionals would read it too. And professionals, even my own audiologist who fit me with hearing aids for many years, have said it opened their eyes too. But I have to tell you, when I wrote the book, I thought I was so unique. Over time, as I heard from more and more people who had read *Hear Again*, I discovered that I am not so unique after all! As a matter of fact, I would say the book is practically a case study about how hearing loss affects a human being. The details may change, but I know from the feedback that people really do identify with the situations and the descriptions.

I think you hit the nail on the head and I think that's why the book is so valuable. When I read it I was really touched by it. I have normal hearing but I've been working with hearing impaired patients for 20 years and there was a commonality in the book that cuts across socioeconomic lines. I think of it as a typical story of how things go when you embark upon obtaining a cochlear implant. It's a nice day-by-day telling of the story and I think that many people can relate to it, and many more will.

I never expected the book would have such an impact on people's lives, so I hope that more people will learn about it and read it themselves. I also hope that professionals will read it and recommend it to their patients. I know from experience that it answers many of the questions that people have about cochlear implants. It's also important to mention that I do point out in the book that how a person functions with a cochlear implant will depend on one's own unique hearing history. I'm thrilled with the way the cochlear implant has impacted my life, and it's my fondest wish to have others understand what cochlear implants can do as well.

Lastly, I think it's important to mention that you actually have no financial stake in the book—is that right?

Correct. I don't gain financially from this. This book was originally published by The League for the Hard of Hearing, and all proceeds have been donated to the League, a wonderful non-profit agency that has helped me and so many others cope with hearing loss.

Thanks so much for your time. I really want to encourage people to read the book, and I thank you for writing it!

Advocates of Cochlear Implants Attempt to Destroy Deaf Culture

Kristina Flores

In the following viewpoint, sociology student Kristina Flores asserts that the hearing world has over time been trying to destroy the "DEAF-WORLD"—Flores's term for the deaf community—through such tactics as mainstreaming deaf children into regular school classrooms and creating hearing devices such as cochlear implants. Flores discusses the eugenics movements of the past in which hearing people discouraged deaf people from gathering, socializing, and reproducing. She feels that any attempt to prevent a hearing-impaired individual to become a part of the deaf community and learn American Sign Language is equivalent to the eugenics of the early twentieth century.

Just like members of other minorities, such as Hispanics and African-Americans, Deaf people experience some of the same oppression and hardships. Although the attempts to "fix" members of and obliterate the DEAF-WORLD are not as highly publicized as problems with other minorities, they still exist. Throughout time, hearing people have been trying to destroy the DEAF-WORLD with the eugenics movement, the mainstreaming of Deaf children into public hearing schools, and cochlear implants.

Eugenics and Deaf Culture

Overall, the eugenics movement was meant to discourage Deaf people from socializing, intermarrying, and reproducing with each other. But these goals are very much unachievable. When

Kristina Flores, "Eradicating the DEAF-WORLD," Delmar College Honors Program Student Creations. www.delmar.edu/socsci/rlong/creation/kristina.htm. Reproduced by permission of the author.

Deaf children are growing up in a residential school, they have no choice but to socialize with other Deaf children. Since they all pretty much use the same language, socialization is not a problem for them. Because these children grow up with others who use their language, they tend to remain close to their friends and often intermarry. Many people, including A. G. [Alexander Graham] Bell [whose experiments with hearing devices led to the invention of the telephone], were opposed to Deaf marrying other Deaf. Bell said that sign language "causes the intermarriage of deaf-mutes and the propagation of their physical defect." Bell also claimed that society was condoning the spread of "a defective race of human beings" by allowing Deaf people to socialize with each other. Since others too saw deafness as a physical defect, they agreed with Bell and started adopting oral schools for the Deaf where signed language was prohibited. If oral schools ended up being the only schools for Deaf, then their signed languages would have diminished along with a part of their heritage and culture. A long time ago, many laws were passed that discouraged Deaf from marrying and reproducing. Even though the percentage of Deaf children born to Deaf families is far less than that of Deaf children born to hearing parents, the fact remains that people believed that Deaf marriages produced Deaf children. So the fact that laws were passed to sterilize Deaf people shows again the attempts to do away with Deaf people and the DEAF-WORLD. Even as recently as 1992, researchers at Boston University claimed to find the gene responsible for a common type of inherited deafness. The director essentially stated that these findings would lead to genetic engineering, which in essence, would eradicate many Deaf people. These researchers want to insert genetic material to prevent hereditary hearing impairment. Really, they want to stop deafness before it starts. The eugenics movement takes on many forms, but they are all aimed at destroying the DEAF-WORLD.

Mainstreaming and Deafness

Mainstreaming Deaf children into hearing public schools, with or without interpreters, has the potential to abolish the DEAF-WORLD. A Deaf child's natural language is American Sign Language [ASL]. Therefore, they should be exposed to and taught as much ASL in school as possible. When Deaf children are mainstreamed into public schools, they lose contact with other Deaf children with whom they can associate and sign with. Many Deaf adults have remained friends with people they met while attending residential schools. For parents that have children with other disabilities, mainstreaming has an inherent attraction, but the movement has caused disruptions in the education of Deaf children. Deaf students cannot be compared with any other group of students. They do not regard themselves as handicapped, but as a linguistic and cultural minority, who have the need and right to go to school together and to live in a community with others of their kind. If mainstreaming were to become standard for educating Deaf children, residential schools would no longer be needed. Then, those important bonds and friendships that were once made only at residential schools cannot be made at all. Mainstreaming Deaf children delays language acquisition because unlike hearing children, the Deaf children cannot hear what the teacher is teaching and cannot just pick things up like hearing children can. The Deaf child must rely on the interpreter, if there is even one present. Right now, there is a shortage of interpreters all over. If all Deaf children were mainstreamed, the shortage would increase and the majority of the children would be in a hearing classroom with no interpreter. The fact that mainstreaming has been happening and will continue to happen is contributing to the eradication of the DEAF-WORLD; Deaf children need to be with other children who use the same language and can share in the same experiences. If children are mainstreamed, they are being deprived of the opportunities to learn about Deaf culture and Deaf heritage.

Placing a Deaf child into a classroom where he can see that he is different from the other children may have some psychological effects on the child. That child should be around other children like themselves. It can boost self-esteem and make learning easier if they are in a more comfortable, natural environment. Mainstreaming Deaf children into public schools can rob them of the chance to learn and grow up in a place rich in Deaf culture and values, such as a residential school. Story telling in American Sign Language is a huge part of sharing culture at residential schools. As in other cultures, stories are carriers of history and vital means of teaching the wisdom of the group for those who do not have Deaf families. If Deaf children do not grow up instilled with Deaf values and knowledge of their culture, then the hearing world is one step closer to stamping out the DEAF-WORLD.

The Threat of Cochlear Implants

Cochlear implants are probably the most well known devices for the destruction of the DEAF-WORLD. A cochlear implant is an electronic device that is surgically implanted in the inner ear. It converts sound to electrical signals that in turn stimulate the auditory nerve. Medical professionals, who are almost always uneducated about other options for Deaf children, often tell parents to have their child receive cochlear implants so the child will be more "normal." Since the vast majority of Deaf children are born to hearing parents, they are also uneducated about the options for their Deaf child. They trust the medical professionals to tell them what to do. The doctors want to "fix" Deaf people by inserting the cochlear implants. The main purpose of the implant is to move the child out of a linguistic and cultural minority and into the majority culture. Essentially, doctors and those who defend the implant are supporting the eradication of all Deaf people. If every child had the implant, then eventually (in the doctors' perfect world) there would be no Deaf people. But this is unrealistic and ridiculous. In the Deaf Community, the cochlear implant is perceived as especially agonizing because unlike hearing aids that can easily be taken off, cochlear implants are surgically implanted. Many Deaf adults see the implants as an affront to their self-worth and they are deemed offensive to their culture. In 1995, the World Federation of the Deaf stated that, ". . . cochlear implants will not help the language acquisition of a Deaf child and can harm the emotional/psychological personality development and physical development." This statement comes from people who know about Deaf people and Deaf culture. The risks dealing with the implant far outweigh the benefits. In fact, after ten years of experimentation with the implants with over a thousand children, not one single case has been reported of a child acquiring oral language with the implant. Implanted children have trouble learning English and ASL both. These children might fall between the two cultures and have none that is really their own. If the implants continue to be inserted into the Deaf, the most distinguishing characteristic of Deaf people, the fact that they cannot hear, will become more and more obsolete until the DEAF-WORLD will no longer exist.

So, the hearing world's attempts to eradicate the DEAF-WORLD have been numerous. But maybe there is a reason the hearing world has not been successful in their attempts. The DEAF-WORLD has a long, rich, and interesting history that should not and cannot be eliminated. The eugenics movement, mainstreaming, and cochlear implants have yet to prove that the culture of Deaf people can be taken away from them, which is ultimately a wonderful thing.

Preventing Puberty in Children with Severe Disabilities Improves Quality of Life

Ashley's Mom and Dad

In the following selection, the authors discuss their belief that they have a right to prevent puberty in their child with severe disabilities. The parents detail their love and affection for their daughter Ashley and their decision to prevent her puberty. Given Ashley's severe disabilities, they feel it would be beneficial for her to remain small and not develop the discomforts associated with the onset of puberty. They deny accusations that Ashley's treatment was undertaken for the convenience of her parents.

Our daughter Ashley had a normal birth, but her mental and motor faculties did not develop. Over the years, neurologists, geneticists, and other specialists conducted every known traditional and experimental test, but still could not determine a diagnosis or a cause. Doctors call her condition "static encephalopathy of unknown etiology," which means an insult to the brain of unknown origin or cause, and one that will not improve.

Now nine years old, Ashley cannot keep her head up, roll or change her sleeping position, hold a toy, or sit up by herself, let alone walk or talk. She is tube fed and depends on her caregivers in every way. We call her our Pillow Angel since she is so sweet and stays right where we place her—usually on a pillow.

Ashley is a beautiful girl whose body is developing normally with no external deformities. She is expected to live a

Ashley's Mom and Dad, "The 'Ashley Treatment' Towards a Better Quality of Life for 'Pillow Angels'," http://ashleytreatment.spaces.live.com/blog, March 25, 2007. Reproduced by permission.

full life and was expected to attain a normal adult height and weight. Ashley being in a stable condition is a blessing because many kids with similarly severe disabilities tend to deteriorate and not survive beyond five years of age.

Ashley is alert and aware of her environment; she startles easily. She constantly moves her arms and kicks her legs. Sometimes she seems to be watching TV intently. She loves music and often gets in celebration mode of vocalizing, kicking, and choreographing/conducting with her hands when she really likes a song ([operatic tenor] Andrea Boccelli is her favorite—we call him her boyfriend). She rarely makes eye-contact even when it is clear that she is aware of a person's presence next to her. Ashley goes to school in a classroom for special needs children, which provides her with daily bus trips, activities customized for her, and a high level of attention by her teachers and therapists.

A Family View

Ashley brings a lot of love to our family and is a bonding factor in our relationship; we can't imagine life without her. She has a sweet demeanor and often smiles and expresses delight when we visit with her, we think she recognizes us but can't be sure. She has a younger healthy sister and brother. We constantly feel the desire to visit her room (her favorite place with special lights and colorful displays) or have her with us wanting to be in her aura of positive energy. We're often gathered around her holding her hand, thus sensing a powerful connection with her pure, innocent and angelic spirit. As often as we can we give her position changes and back rubs, sweet talk her, move her to social and engaging places, and manage her entertainment setting (music or TV). In return she inspires abundant love in our hearts, so effortlessly; she is such a blessing in our life!

To express how intensely we feel about providing Ashley with the best care possible, we would like to quote from a private email that we received from a loving mother with her own 6 year old Pillow Angel: "In my mind, I have to be immortal because I have to always be here on Earth to take care of my precious child. Taking care of him is difficult, but it is never a burden. I am [his] eyes, ears and voice. He is my best friend, and I have dedicated my life to providing joy and comfort to him. To my last breath, everything I will ever do will be for him or because of him. I cannot adequately put into words the amount of love and devotion I have for my child. I am sure that you feel the same way about Ashley."

The chance of Ashley having significant improvement, such as being able to change her position in bed, let alone walk, is non-existent. She has been at the same level of cognitive, mental and physical developmental ability since about three months of age. Ashley has aged and grown in size but her mental and physical abilities have remained and will remain those of an infant.

Faced with Ashley's medical reality, as her deeply loving parents, we worked with her doctors to do all we could to provide Ashley with the best possible quality of life. The result is the "Ashley Treatment."

The Medical Treatment

The Ashley Treatment is the name we have given to a collection of medical procedures for the improvement of Ashley's quality of life. The treatment includes growth attenuation through high-dose estrogen therapy, hysterectomy to eliminate the menstrual cycle and associated discomfort to Ashley, and breast bud removal to avoid the development of large breasts and the associated discomfort to Ashley. We pursued this treatment after much thought, research, and discussions with doctors.

Nearly three years after we started this process, and after the treatment was published in October 2006 by Dr. [Daniel] Gunther and Dr. [Douglas] Diekema in a medical journal that resulted in an extensive and worldwide coverage by the press and dozens of public discussions, we decided to share our thoughts and experience for two purposes: first, to help families who might bring similar benefits to their bedridden Pillow Angels; second, to address some misconceptions about the treatment and our motives for undertaking it.

A fundamental and universal misconception about the treatment is that it is intended to convenience the caregiver; rather, the central purpose is to improve Ashley's quality of life. Ashley's biggest challenges are discomfort and boredom; all other considerations in this discussion take a back seat to these central challenges. The Ashley Treatment goes right to the heart of these challenges and we strongly believe that it will mitigate them in a significant way and provide Ashley with lifelong benefits.

The Best Solution

Unlike what most people thought, the decision to pursue the Ashley Treatment was not a difficult one. Once we understood the options, problems, and benefits, the right course was clear to us. Ashley will be a lot more physically comfortable free of menstrual cramps, free of the discomfort associated with large and fully-developed breasts, and with a smaller, lighter body that is better suited to constant lying down and is easier to be moved around.

Ashley's smaller and lighter size makes it more possible to include her in the typical family life and activities that provide her with needed comfort, closeness, security and love: meal time, car trips, touch, snuggles, etc. Typically, when awake, babies are in the same room as other family members, the sights and sounds of family life engaging the baby's attention, entertaining the baby. Likewise, Ashley has all of a baby's needs, including being entertained and engaged, and she calms at the sounds of family voices. Furthermore, given Ashley's mental age, a nine and a half year old body is more appropriate and provides her more dignity and integrity than a fully grown female body.

Preventing Puberty in Children with Severe Disabilities Is a Violation of Personal Rights

Disability Rights Education and Defense Fund

The following viewpoint expresses the Disability Rights Education and Defense Fund's position against parents choosing to prevent puberty in their disabled children. Although the fund empathizes with parents raising children with severe disabilities, it feels that preventing puberty violates the child's human rights. The authors of the statement call on members of the community to support and help parents of the disabled so that the violation of disabled children's rights can be averted. The Disability Rights Education and Defense Fund is a national civil rights law and policy center that defends the rights of the disabled through legal action, education, training, public policy, and legislative action.

"Benevolence" and "good intentions" have often had disastrous consequences for the disability community. Throughout history, "for their own good" has motivated and justified discrimination against us. The recent story about nine-year-old Ashley, a child with severe disabilities, exemplifies this problem. When she was six, Ashley's parents requested that their daughter be treated with medications (large doses of estrogen) to halt her physical growth, and with surgeries to remove her breasts and uterus.

These interventions were undertaken at the Children's Hospital of the University of Washington, School of Medicine in Seattle, after consultations with the medical center's ethics committee.

Disability Rights Education and Defense Fund, "Modify the System, Not the Person," http://dredf.org, January 7, 2007. Reproduced by permission.

An article about the case appeared in the October 2006 issue of *Archives of Pediatrics and Adolescent Medicine* and MSNBC first reported the story on November 1, 2006. Ashley is now nine years old, with an expected final height of 4'5" and a weight of 75 pounds. The physicians involved with Ashley's care have expressed the opinion that she will never achieve a cognitive level greater than that of a three-month-old. Ashley's parents, who call her their "Pillow Angel," argue that they can care for her more easily if she remains permanently small, and that she as well as they will benefit from these medical interventions. The case was reported by the *Los Angeles Times*, the Associated Press, CNN, and many other media outlets on January 4 [2007], and it has since raised a firestorm of debate.

Autonomy Must Be Honored

We deeply empathize with parents who face difficult issues raising children with significant physical and intellectual disabilities. However, we hold as non-negotiable the principle that personal and physical autonomy of all people with disabilities be regarded as sacrosanct. For decades, parents, families, and the disability community have been fighting for this principle, and for community-based services for children and adults that make it a reality. Their advocacy led to enactment of state and federal laws in the 1970s that establish extensive rights to full personhood for children and adults with disabilities. These laws were passed to remedy our shameful history of abuse and mistreatment of people just like Ashley.

As parents and adults with disabilities, our experience demonstrates unequivocally that all people with disabilities can be an integral part of home and community, if needed help and support is available. It is not always easy to find home care workers who are competent and empathetic. Too often, we must fight to persuade social service and healthcare bureaucracies that help at home and appropriate equipment such as adapted wheelchairs and mechanical lifts are essential and fundamental to our autonomy.

However, if these problems seem insurmountable, or cannot as a practical matter be surmounted, as Ashley's parents suggest, then it is all our duty to change the system so it works rather than find novel ways to modify people so that they will more easily "fit" a flawed system.

Support for the Disabled

Where, we wonder, was the network of programs and services that exist in every state when Ashley's family decided the best option was to employ medical procedures that violated their daughter's autonomy and personhood? Were other families whose children have disabilities like Ashley's asked to talk about their experiences and how they solved problems as their children grew to adulthood?

Where were the social workers and advocates who should be providing alternative perspectives? Why did the system fail this family and their daughter? That, it seems to us, is a fundamental question.

Ethical Violations

Beyond these apparent institutional failures, the conduct of Ashley's physicians and the ethics committee's decision in this tragic story should be widely questioned—there are future implications for other families and their children who have significant impairments. We rely on healthcare professionals to alleviate pain and suffering and maintain functionality, not decide when someone is worthy of holding human rights. After decades of struggle to enshrine the human rights of people with disabilities in law and policy and to challenge the overwhelming prejudice, negative attitudes, and misperceptions that are widely held about people with intellectual disabilities, this sad and puzzling episode must not mark a turning point for those hard-won gains.

It is ironic in light of this story that the United Nations General Assembly recently adopted the first convention of the twenty-first century—the Convention on the Protection and Promotion of the Rights and Dignity of Persons with Disabilities.

Recognizing that the rights of people with disabilities to autonomy and personhood are still violated by many nations around the world. Article 17 of the Convention, entitled "Protecting the integrity of the person," reads, "Every person with disabilities has a right to respect for his or her physical and mental integrity on an equal basis with others." In our view, Ashley has been denied her basic human rights through draconian interventions to her person.

Prenatal Genetic Testing Prevents Diseases and Disabilities

Johann Hari

In the following selection, British journalist and writer Johann Hari discusses his support of genetic testing prior to birth. Hari notes that preimplantation genetic diagnosis makes it possible for parents to avoid having children with severe and life-threatening disabilities. He argues that genetic testing before birth does not detract from the value of people with disabilities; instead he feels that testing acknowledges that it is easier to live the type of life desired if one is not disabled. In Hari's opinion prenatal and preimplantation genetic testing is designed to produce healthier babies and is employed by parents motivated by love.

A decade after the creation of Dolly the sheep [the first animal to be cloned], we are living in a glorious age of liberation biology. New technologies are unveiled by doctors almost every week that make it possible to reduce the sum of human suffering in ways that would have seemed like *Star Trek* science-fiction when she first came mewing into our world.

Genetic Testing Before Birth

Preimplantation Genetic Diagnosis makes it possible for couples with terrible hereditary diseases to have children without condemning them to a life of suffering. Stem cell research makes it possible for people with ruined spines to have some hope that they may walk again. Genetic screening has ensured hundreds of children are alive today because "saviour siblings"

Johann Hari, "Why I Support Liberal Eugenics," *The Independent* (London), July 6, 2006, p. 29. Copyright © 2006 Independent Newspapers (UK) Ltd. Reproduced by permission.

were created as a match. Some time soon, infertile couples may be able to produce clones to pass on their genes. Human life is being extended and enhanced in ways that spread joy and harm no one.

Leon Kass, the chairman of George [W.] Bush's Council of Bioethics, recently summarised some of these, the greatest biological advances of our time: "The Pill. In vitro fertilisation [IVF]. Bottled embryos. Surrogate wombs. Cloning. Genetic screening. Genetic manipulation. Organ harvesting. Mechanical spare parts. Brain implants. Ritalin for the young, Viagra for the old, Prozac for everyone. And, to leave this vale of tears, a little extra Morphine accompanied by Muzak."

Condemning Scientific Advances

But Kass was not offering this as a joyous hymn of praise. No—he was offering it as a condemnation. He is not alone. There is a large constituency of people scattered across the world who treat the doctors pioneering these treatments as moral criminals. Amazing though it might seem, they want to stop all human beings from using technologies that will make our children healthier, cleverer and less likely to be disabled. This movement of bio-Luddites stretches from the White House to radical disability activists to the Vatican, and if the decent pro-science majority do not fight back, they will win.

To understand what this will mean, we need to look at what would have happened if the bio-conservatives had prevailed a generation ago. The very same people described doctors who performed the first organ transplants as "body snatchers" and "grave robbers". They predicted that the sickly would swiftly be bumped off in their hospital beds to harvest their hearts and livers and lungs. If they had won, tens of thousands of the people reading this article would be dead. When IVF went mainstream, people like Leon Kass said it was "playing God" to conceive a child in a test tube, and that the relationship between children and parents would be "irreparably damaged". If they had prevailed, tens of thousands of the people reading this would not exist.

Kass still says we should heed the "urgh!" factor, and trust "the wisdom of our own repugnance". But pre-rational repugnance quickly fades once we see the life-enhancing benefits of new technologies. So are there any more sensible objections to these life-extending therapies, and how can they be answered?

The Vatican [headquarters of the Roman Catholic Church], and some other religious authorities argue that at the moment of conception, an invisible supernatural agent ("God") implants an invisible substance ("a soul") into a cluster of cells smaller than a speck of dust, and from that moment on the cells are a person with inalienable rights. To perform tests on them is morally equivalent to performing tests on an adult human. Discarded embryos have been murdered. This view is given a privileged place on the world stage.

To a materialist who rejects supernatural explanations for the world, this is not tenable. We believe humans develop in stages, and that they have far greater rights once they become self-aware and capable of feeling pain—at about 12 weeks after conception—than when they are insentient blobs with no brains or feelings at all. During a fire in a biotech lab, would anybody really rescue a petri dish containing two embryos before they saved Steven Hawking? Yet that is the warped moral choice dictated by Catholic theology.

The Position of the Disabled

The criticism that deserves more careful consideration comes from disability rights activists like Adrienne Asch. They argue that this attempt to eradicate disability is an assault on disabled people. By trying to eradicate disabilities, we are saying disabled people are worth less—"errors in the gene pool"—and clearing the way for them to be treated even more badly.

But is this true? By making sure that no more mothers take thalidomide [a drug that causes deformities in offspring] during pregnancy, are we implicitly saying that thalidomide people have worthless lives and should be killed? Of course not. We are simply saying that a person is more likely to be able to live the kind of life they want to with fully formed arms and legs. By ensuring that the number of able-bodied babies are maximised, we are simply acknowledging that— however harsh it might seem to say it—lacking an ability to hear or see or walk is not simply a difference. It is a disability nobody would voluntarily choose, and that you are better off without. Nor does the evidence suggest greater screening and treatment will lead to the remaining disabled people being treated worse. Since amniocentesis was introduced, people with Down syndrome are, if anything, treated better.

A World Divided

The only criticism that really lingers in the mind comes from egalitarian critics. They warn that human biotechnology may create a world divided between the rich, with their "Genetically Modified Babies", and the poor, who are lumbered with the random flaws of nature. The idea of human equality will, they say, melt in the biotech labs. But there are already inequalities thrown up by nature.

I am nowhere near as clever as [economist] Amartya Sen, nor as good-looking as, say, the average tub of lard. Does that mean human equality is a nonsense? No—my belief in it is strong enough to cope with smarter, fitter people. The solution to unequal access to biotech cannot be the [Communist leader Joseph] Stalin-style leveling down proposed by the biotech-banners. We did not react to the invention of medicine—which similarly benefited only the rich at first—by banning it. We reacted by creating the NHS [National Health Service of the United Kingdom] so everyone could access it.

None of these worries outweigh the benefits of biotechnology. We should be honest enough to call this attempt to improve the genetic lot of humanity by its name—liberal eugenics. It has nothing to do with the evil of Nazi eugenics, which was imposed by the state and concerned not with producing healthier babies but with deranged race theories. No, this new brand is voluntarily entered into by parents, and it is motivated by love, not hate.

The risk of not following this path—and failing to uncover cures for a thousand curses on humanity—is far greater than the risk of acting. Those who want to stop these natural, beautiful acts of love should be shunned and shamed.

This has nothing to do with the evils of Nazi eugenics. It is entered into by parents and it is motivated by love.

Prenatal Genetic Testing Ignores the Value of People with Disabilities

Elizabeth R. Schiltz

In the following viewpoint, Elizabeth R. Schiltz, a parent of a child with Down syndrome, voices her concern that prenatal testing is an assault on the value of the disabled. Schiltz equates the prenatal testing process with the Nazi programs of euthanizing people with disabilities. She raises concerns that parents who knowingly choose to give birth to a child affected by a disability diagnosed prenatally may make them financially liable and shunned by society.

When I was about five months pregnant with my third child, Peter, I . . . had prenatal testing using amniotic fluid extracted from my womb by a big needle during a procedure called amniocentesis. The [results indicated] . . . that Petey's cells have *three*, rather than the usual two, copies of chromosome number 21. This indicates that he has an incurable chromosomal condition called Trisomy 21, or Down Syndrome, or in the quaint, old-fashioned language of the Nazi regime, "mongolism."

A Seek-and-Destroy Mission

The medical professionals I was dealing with through these tests were not trying to find information to help me protect the health of my baby. Unlike anemia or HIV [human immunodeficiency virus that causes AIDS], there is little that can be done about the conditions that these tests were designed to

Elizabeth R. Schiltz, "Living in the Shadow of Mönchberg," *The Cost of "Choice": Women Evaluate the Impact of Abortion*, New York: Encounter Books, 2004, pp. 42–49.
Copyright © 2004 by Erika Bachiochi. All rights reserved. Reproduced by permission by the publisher, Encounter Books, San Francisco, CA. www.encounterbooks.com.

identify. They were offered for the purpose of bestowing upon me a special societal privilege to choose to abort my baby. That karyotype [a cell's chromosomal characteristic] could have been my ticket to a guilt-free, utterly justified, absolutely legal abortion—even five months into my pregnancy. If the technology had existed in the 1940s, that karyotype would almost certainly have been Petey's ticket to the concentration camp Hadamar.

As someone who has always been pro-life, I did not accept these tests for the purpose of obtaining that "privilege." I just wanted to know, partly in the hope that I could be reassured that nothing was wrong, but also so that, if I could not be reassured, I could at least be prepared. I am a nerd. If I was going to have a baby with Down Syndrome, I wanted to read every book on the subject before the baby arrived.

Insights into Prenatal Testing

Experiencing this testing sequence firsthand, however, gave me some insights into the potentially pernicious effects of the prenatal testing process. The tests are all offered in the guise of "reassurance." They all carry with them the implication that the responsible mother can and should do something constructive with the results: take extra iron if she is found to be anemic, take [the drug] AZT if she has HIV, abort the baby if he has Down Syndrome. If you lack the financial or other resources to raise a child with a disability, you could easily be swayed by an argument that the knowledge you now possess about the child gives you the responsibility to do something constructive to solve the problem—by doing away with the child.

Now, this argument could obviously be a powerful incentive for a person to choose an abortion. Going through this process personally made me acutely aware of its power. But this was not the aspect of the experience that really *surprised* me. What surprised me was that people did not stop making this argument once I had rejected it during the testing phase. When I started telling people that the baby I was expecting would have Down Syndrome, colleagues asked me incredulously, "Why are you having this baby?" While there was something rather creepy about being asked that question directly, by someone staring at that big belly of mine while the baby kicked inside, it was still not so difficult for me to deal with. I was comfortable defending my position that I didn't believe in abortion, that I didn't think I had any choice in this matter; I was still in familiar, pro-life territory.

Questions from Society

But I left that familiar territory the moment Petey was born, and I found, to my astonishment, that society still kept asking that question—why did you have this baby? I have seen people react with marked surprise when they hear that I knew Petey would have Down Syndrome before he was born. Though they do not ask aloud, you can see the question in their eyes: "If you knew, why did you have the baby?" What's buried in that question, deep in their eyes, is the perception of my son as a "choice"—specifically, *my* choice—rather than a unique human being created in God's image, a full-fledged member of the human race.

Child Versus Cost

What I see in their eyes is the lingering shadow of Mönchberg [referring to the German city of Mönchberg, where in 1940 the Nazi regime established a hospital for the purpose of exterminating people with disabilities] that sometimes keeps me awake at night. I worry that the availability of abortion seems to be eroding societal consensus about our collective responsibility for vulnerable people—those with disabilities that were or could have been diagnosed prenatally, or even people born into difficult family situations or social structures. I am very frightened by the emerging attitude that if a woman exercises her "choice" to have a child who can be identified in advance as "vulnerable" for some reason, the woman herself bears full responsibility for dealing with that vulnerability. In other words, if the "cost" of a certain life is going to be more than its "worth," someone has to make up the deficit. *If you "choose" to impose that cost on society by having a baby you could so easily have aborted, you should pay the price.*

Examples of this attitude abound. Bob Edwards, the scientist who created Great Britain's first *in vitro* fertilization baby, recently gave a speech at an international fertility conference in France in which he expressed just this view. He opined: "Soon it will be a sin of parents to have a child that carries the heavy burden of genetic disease. We are entering a world where we have to consider the quality of our children." In other words, if we can identify a genetic condition before a child is born, and the parents choose to have the baby anyway, *they are committing a sin.* They're making a choice that society is going to have to pay for. *It is their choice—their sin. They should have to pay. . . .*

This same attitude lurks behind the increasing number of wrongful birth and wrongful life lawsuits being brought all over the United States. In these suits, parents of children with disabilities (typically Down Syndrome) sue medical professionals for failing to diagnose the condition correctly before birth. The parents argue that they would have aborted the children, and thus "solved" the problem, if they had known about the condition. But since they were not given that option, they should not have to bear the costs; instead, the medical professionals who denied them their "choice" should pay. In other words, the "problem" is the fault of some identifiable person—this case, a medical professional. That person, rather than society at large, should thus bear the cost. . . .

Designer Babies

This same attitude also underlies the growing trend of creating designer babies by artificially fertilizing embryos and then conducting pre-implantation genetic screening in order to select only the embryos that lack certain problematic genes, or that have certain features, such as bone marrow tissue suitable for transplant to an ill sibling, or the desired sex. Garland F. Allen, a historian of science, recently wrote an article in *Science* magazine comparing the social conditions that supported the spread of the eugenics movement in the early part of the twentieth century with the social conditions of today. He expressed a fear that they are the same, and he claimed, "As health care costs skyrocket, we are coming to accept a bottom-line, cost-benefit analysis of human life." We can now create "perfect" babies. We can also abort less-than-perfect babies. *It is a matter of choice—your choice, Mom. If you choose to keep that less-than-perfect baby, that is your choice, but it is also your problem. You could have solved it for us. You chose not to. So you pay for that choice.*

Quality of Life

Those who would adhere to a cost-benefit analysis of the lives of people with disabilities have to admit serious problems in determining how such a morally suspect analysis would ever work in practice. Some have attempted to calculate the *cost* of allowing a child with Down Syndrome to be born. Although I am extremely skeptical of such calculations, I suppose, in theory, I could be convinced that a rough economic analysis *might* allow some generalizations, at least about the *financial* costs of raising a hypothetically typical child with Down Syndrome. But what possible criteria could be rationally imposed to quantify the *benefit* of such a life? Whose calculation of the benefit could one trust? Should we ask the people who really ought to know—people who live with disabilities? After all, disability rights activists maintain that "most people with disabilities rate their quality of life as much higher than other people think. People make the decision [to reject embryos] based on a prejudice that having a disability means having a low quality of life."

Should we ask parents raising children with disabilities? *The Child Who Never Grew*, Pulitzer and Nobel Prize–winning author Pearl S. Buck, is a beautiful book about one such parent's experiences. Ms. Buck eloquently describes the heartbreak and sorrow she experienced in raising a daughter who was mentally retarded as a result of a metabolic condition called PKU (phenylketonuria). But she also describes some of the benefits:

> [B]y this most sorrowful way I was compelled to tread, I learned respect and reverence for every human mind. It was my child who taught me to understand so clearly that all people are equal in their humanity and that all have the same human rights. None is to be considered less, as a human being, than any other, and each must be given his place and his safety in the world. I might never have learned this in any other way. I might have gone on in the arrogance of my own intolerance for those less able than myself. My child taught me humanity.

How can we possibly determine the market value of such lessons? What tuition would we charge for learning humanity?

Despite its methodological flaws, the "bottom-line, cost-benefit analysis of human life" clearly has become generally accepted in many spheres of our society. Can anything be done to dispel this dark and sinister shadow of Mönchberg's smoke cloud?

Counterstrike Against Eugenics

In the end, the cost-benefit attitude toward the lives of those with special vulnerability will have to be countered by an attitude that is deeper and stronger—and much more American. University of Georgia professor Edward Larson, winner of the 1998 Pulitzer Prize in history, authored a book in 1995 about the rise and fall of eugenic sterilization in the southern United States in the early part of the last century. In conclusion, he wrote: "At least in the Deep South, values founded on traditional religion and concern for individual rights served as more effective protection against the excesses of eugenics than did any internal regulatory mechanism within medicine or science."

Values founded on the concern for individual rights, like the conviction articulated in our Declaration of Independence: "that all men are created equal, that they are endowed by their Creator with certain inalienable Rights, that among these are Life, Liberty and the pursuit of Happiness."

Values founded on traditional religion, like the statement from the Apostle Paul:

> The body is one and has many members, but all the members, so many though they are, are one body. . . . If the body were all eye, what would happen to our hearing? If it were all ear, what would happen to our smelling? As it is, God has set each member of the body in the place he wanted it to be. If all the members were alike, where would the body be? . . . Even those members of the body which seem less important are in fact indispensable.

These values are not empty platitudes. They are the foundations of our republic and our conception of democracy. These values must be forcefully asserted in each and every context in which anyone attempts, through a cost-benefit analysis, to adjudge any human life as not worthy of living.

Chronology

546–371 BC

Several ancient societies including the Athenians, the Spartans, and the Romans have laws and societal practices that mandate the death of newborns born with birth defects.

355 BC

Aristotle asserts that individuals born deaf become senseless and incapable of reason.

313 BC

Emperor Constantine abolishes infanticide (the killing of unwanted infants) in ancient Rome after his conversion to Christianity.

1500s

Physician Girolamo Cardano (1501–1576) recognizes the ability of deaf people to reason.

1598–1601

People with disabilities are forced to beg using a cap to collect donations, leading to the term "handicapped."

1755

Charles Michel Abbe del'Epee establishes the first free school for the deaf.

1800s

Disabilities are believed to be caused solely by genetics.

1800s

Traveling shows and circuses commonly display people with physical disabilities in "freak" shows.

1817

The American School for the Deaf is founded in Hartford, Connecticut. It is the first school for disabled children in the United States.

1848

The first residential institution for people with mental retardation is founded at the Perkins Institution in Boston.

1860

Dr. Simon Pollak demonstrates the use of braille, a system of writing and reading by touching raised dots, at the Missouri School for the Blind.

1869

The first wheelchair patent is registered with the U.S. Patent Office.

1883

Sir Francis Galton creates the term "eugenics" to describe his suggestions to create a better society by controlled matings to produce children and to prevent people with disabilities from having children.

1900s

Increased social responsibility occurs as a result of men returning from World War I and World War II with physical disabilities.

1912

Henry H. Goddard publishes a best-selling book in which he links disability with immorality and alleging that both are tied to genetics.

1921

The U.S. Supreme Court, in *Buck v. Bell*, rules that the forced sterilization of people with disabilities is not a violation of their constitutional rights.

1933

Franklin Delano Roosevelt takes office as the first physically disabled U.S. president.

1935

The U.S. Congress passes the Social Security Act, which establishes federal old-age benefits and assistance to blind individuals and children with disabilities.

1935

The League of the Physically Handicapped is formed in New York City to protest discrimination against people with disabilities by federal programs.

1937

A U.S. poll finds that 45 percent of individuals favor euthanasia for "defective infants."

1945

President Harry Truman establishes "Employ the Handicapped Week."

1948

The disabled students' program at the University of Illinois at Galesburg is established.

1949

The first Annual Wheelchair Basketball Tournament is held in Galesburg, Illinois.

1950

The United Cerebral Palsy Association joins with the Association for Retarded Children, taking a major advocacy role in the "Parents' Movement" of the 1950s.

1951

Dr. Howard Rusk opens the Institute of Rehabilitation Medicine at New York University Medical Center, which begins work on innovative, adaptive aids for people with severe disabilities.

1960

The first Paralympic Games are held in Rome.

1961

President John F. Kennedy appoints a special President's Panel on Mental Retardation, to investigate the status of people with mental retardation and develop programs and reforms for its improvement.

1965

Medicare and Medicaid are established to provide federally subsidized health care to the disabled and elderly Americans.

1966

President Lyndon Johnson establishes the President's Committee on Mental Retardation.

1966

Burton Batt and Fred Kaplan publish *Christmas in Purgatory*, which documents the appalling conditions at state institutions for people with developmental disabilities.

1968

The Architectural Barriers Act is passed, mandating that federally constructed buildings and facilities be accessible to people with physical disabilities.

1968

The Physically Disabled Students Program is founded by Ed Roberts.

1972

The parents of residents at the Willowbrook State School file suit to end the inhumane conditions at that institution.

1973

The first handicapped parking permits are introduced in Washington, D.C.

1973

The Rehabilitation Act is passed, prohibiting federally funded programs from discriminating against people with disabilities.

1975

The American Coalition of Citizens with Disabilities (ACCD) is established to promote cross-disability advocacy on a national level.

1975

The Education for All Handicapped Children Act is passed, establishing the right of children with disabilities to education.

1977

Disability activists occupy federal buildings in ten cities in protest, compelling implementation of the first federal antidiscrimination legislation.

1982

Parents of a baby with Down syndrome ("Baby Doe") are advised not to pursue lifesaving surgery for the child and so the baby dies. The case stimulates the creation of regulations safeguarding the civil rights of disabled newborns.

1990

The Americans with Disabilities Act is signed by President George H.W. Bush. The law mandates access within reason to local, state, and federal government programs, businesses with more than fifteen employees, restaurants, and stores.

1999

Individuals with Disabilities Education Act (IDEA) mandates a Free Appropriate education to individuals with disabilities.

2001

Compliance with Section 508 of the Rehabilitation Act becomes mandatory throughout the federal government. This requires accessibility of information in venues as varied as information kiosks to parks and Web sites.

2004

Individuals with Disabilities Education Improvement Act (IDEIA) is passed. The act is an expansion on the 1999 IDEA act containing provisions aimed at strengthening how special education students' academic progress is measured.

Organizations to Contact

The editors have compiled the following list of organizations concerned with the issues debated in this book. The descriptions are derived from materials provided by the organizations. All have publications or information available for interested readers. The list was compiled on the date of publication of the present volume; the information provided here may change. Readers need to remember that many organizations take several weeks or longer to respond to inquiries.

American Association of People with Disabilities (AAPD)
629 K St. NW, Ste. 503, Washington, DC   20006
(202) 457-0046
Web site: www.aapd-dc.org

AAPD is the largest national nonprofit cross-disability member organization in the United States, dedicated to ensuring economic self-sufficiency and political empowerment for the more than 50 million Americans with disabilities. AAPD works in coalition with other disability organizations for the full implementation and enforcement of disability nondiscrimination laws, particularly the Americans with Disabilities Act (ADA) of 1990 and the Rehabilitation Act of 1973. The AAPD runs an e-mail-based news network called Justice for All, which defends and advances rights of the disabled.

The Arc
1010 Wayne Ave., Ste. 650, Silver Spring, MD   20910
(301) 565-3842 • fax: (301) 565-3843
Web site: www.thearc.org

The Arc is the world's largest community-based organization of and for people with intellectual and developmental disabilities. It provides services and support for families and individuals and includes over 140,000 members affiliated through more than 850 state and local chapters across the nation. The

Arc is devoted to promoting and improving support and services for all people with intellectual and developmental disabilities. The organization has many publications including fact sheets and a family resource guide.

BC Coalition of People with Disabilities (BCCPD)
204-456 W. Broadway, Vancouver   BC V5Y 1R3
  Canada
(604) 875-0188 • fax: (604) 875-9227
e-mail: feedback@bccpd.bc.ca
Web site: www.bccpd.bc.ca

BCCPD is an organization run by and for people with disabilities throughout British Columbia. Through its work, the coalition promotes the full participation of people with disabilities in all aspects of society. Among its publications are *Transition* magazine, *Disability Benefits Help Sheets*, the *Tips for Living Well* newsletter, and several other position statements and pamphlets.

Cato Institute
1000 Massachusetts Ave. NW, Washington, DC   20001
(202) 842-0200 • fax: (202) 842-3490
Web site: www.cato.org

The Cato Institute is a nonprofit public policy research foundation dedicated to promoting limited government and individual liberty. The institute believes the Americans with Disabilities Act is not effective and imposes unreasonable costs on businesses. It publishes journals, newsletters, and essays as well as numerous position papers, including "Handicapping Freedom: The Americans with Disabilities Act" and "The Unintended Consequences of the Americans with Disabilities Act."

Center for Independent Living (CIL)
2539 Telegraph Ave., Berkeley, CA   94704
(510) 841-4776 • fax: (510) 841-6168
Web site: www.cilberkeley.org

The world's first organization run by and for people with disabilities, the CIL, founded in 1972, supports disabled people in their efforts toward independence. CIL encourages people with disabilities to make their own choices and works to open doors in the community to full participation and access for all.

Center on Human Policy

School of Education, Syracuse University, 805 S. Crouse Ave. Syracuse, NY   13244-2280
(315) 443-3851 • fax: (315) 443-4338
e-mail: thechp@sued.syr.edu
Web site: http://thechp.syr.edu

The center works to promote the full inclusion of people with developmental disabilities in community life. It provides information to families, human services professionals, and others on laws, regulations, and programs affecting children and adults with disabilities. Among the center's publications are a "Community for All" Tool Kit, a declaration of disability rights called the Community Imperative, numerous fact sheets, and books such as *Christmas in Purgatory: A Photographic Essay on Mental Retardation* and *Ordinary Moments: The Disabled Experience.*

Disabled Peoples' International (DPI)

874 Topsail Rd., Mount Pearl, Newfoundland   A1N 3J9
  Canada
(204) 287-8010 • fax: (709) 747-7603
e-mail: dpi@dpi.org
Web site: www.dpi.org

DPI is a development organization established to help disabled people take charge of their lives. It works to achieve equality for disabled people worldwide. Among its numerous publications are several position papers, the quarterly *Disability International,* the paper "From Vision to Action: The Road to Implementation of the Convention on the Rights of Persons with Disabilities," and the book *The Last Civil Rights Movement.*

Disability Rights Education & Defense Fund (DREDF)

2212 Sixth St., Berkeley, CA   94710
(510) 644-2555 (v/tty) • fax: (510) 841-8645
e-mail: info@dredf.org
Web site: www.dredf.org

The DREDF, founded in 1979, is a national civil rights law and policy center directed by individuals with disabilities and parents who have children with disabilities. The mission of the organization is to advance the civil and human rights of people with disabilities through legal advocacy, training, education, and public policy and legislative development. DREDF publishes reports, articles, books, issue papers, handbooks, guides, pamphlets, videos, and other communications are intended to provide information and help on issues affecting people with disabilities.

The Federation for Children with Special Needs (FCSN)

1135 Tremont St., Ste. 420, Boston, MA   02120
(617) 236-7210 • fax: (617) 572-2094
e-mail: fcsninfo@fcsn.org
Web site: http://fcsn.org

FCSN provides information, support, and assistance to parents of children with disabilities, their professional partners, and their communities. They are committed to listening to and learning from families, and encouraging full participation in community life by all people, especially those with disabilities. Publications by the federation include a Literacy Resource Guide for Families and Educators and a directory of parent centers.

Learning Disabilities Association of America (LDA)

4156 Library Rd., Pittsburgh, PA   15234-1349
(412) 341-1515 • fax: (412) 344-0224
Web site: www.ldanatl.org

LDA is a national volunteer organization comprising individuals with learning disabilities, their families, and concerned professionals. It works to alleviate the detrimental effects of learning disabilities and supports research on the causes of learning disabilities. LDA publishes the multidisciplinary journal *Learning Disabilities.*

National Center for Learning Disabilities (NCLD)
381 Park Ave. S, Ste. 1401, New York, NY   10016
(212) 545-7510 • fax: (212) 545-9665
Web site: www.ncld.org

NCLD promotes public awareness and understanding of children and adults with learning disabilities so that they may achieve their potential and enjoy full participation in society. NCLD publishes several online publications including the monthly *LD News.*

National Council on Independent Living (NCIL)
1710 Rhode Island Ave. NW, Washington, D.C.   20036
(202) 207-0334 • fax: (202) 207-0341
e-mail: ncil@tsbbs02.tnet.com
Web site: www.ncil.org

NCIL is the national membership association of local nonprofit corporations known as Independent Living Centers (ILCs). NCIL promotes the full integration and participation of persons with disabilities in society, as well as the development, improvement, and expansion of ILCs. It publishes the *Weekly Advocacy Monitor (WhAM)* and various position papers.

National Information Center for Children and Youth with Disabilities (NICHCY)
PO Box 1492, Washington, D.C.   20013-1492
(202) 884-8200 • fax: (202) 884-8441
e-mail: nichcy@aed.org
Web site: www.kidsource.com/NICHCY

NICHCY is a clearinghouse that provides information on disabilities and related issues. It assists parents, educators, caregivers, advocates, and others in helping children and youth with disabilities to participate as fully as possible in school, at home, and in the community. NICHCY publishes the annual *Disability Fact Sheet* and the periodic newsletter *News Digest*.

National Institute on Developmental Delays (NIDD)

1900 West MacArthur, Shawnee, OK   75801
(405) 878-5301 • fax: (405) 878-5114
e-mail: pop@nidd.org
Web site: www.nidd.org

The NIDD is a national resource center with a global outlook that strives to help children with developmental delays and their families. The resource center publishes articles on child development issues and publishes *CALL News*, a quarterly newsletter.

Reason Foundation

3415 S. Sepulveda Blvd., Ste. 400, Los Angeles, CA   90034
(310) 391-2245 • fax: (310) 391-4395
Web site: www.reason.org

The Reason Foundation is a national public policy research organization that promotes individual freedoms and libertarian principles. It believes that the Americans with Disabilities Act is too expensive to enforce. It publishes numerous publications including the monthly *Privatization Watch* and the magazine *Reason*.

VOR

836 S. Arlington Heights Rd., Ste. 351
Arlington Heights, IL   60007
(847) 399-AVOR • fax: (847) 253-6054
e-mail: tamie327@hotmail.com
Web site: www.vor.net

The goal of VOR, formerly called Voice of the Retarded, is to keep public officials, legislators, and the general public informed about issues that affect persons with mental retardation. It supports alternatives in residential living and rehabilitation systems that best suit the individual needs of people with mental retardation. VOR's publications include the position paper "Voice of the Retarded Statement on Deinstitutionalization."

For Further Research

Books

H-Dirksen L. Bauman, *Open Your Eyes: Deaf Studies Talking*, Minneapolis: University Of Minnesota Press, 2008.

Marcy Joy Epstein and Travar Pettway, *Deep: Real Life with Spinal Cord Injury*, Ann Arbor: University of Michigan Press, 2008.

Kogan Esther, *Pathway to Inclusion: Voices from the Field*, Lanham, MD: University Press of America, 2005.

Donald R. Gallo, ed., *Owning It: Stories About Teens with Disabilities*, Cambridge, MA: Candlewick, 2008.

John Harris, *Enhancing Evolution: The Ethical Case for Making Better People*, Princeton, NJ: Princeton University Press, 2007.

Paul T. Jaeger and Cynthia Ann Bowman, *Understanding Disability: Inclusion, Access, Diversity, and Civil Rights*, Westport, CT: Praeger, 2005.

Jason Kingsley and Mitchell Levitz, *Count Us In: Growing Up with Down Syndrome*, Orlando, FL: Harcourt, 2007.

Melissa Marshall, *Getting It: Persuading Organizations and Individuals to Be More Comfortable with People with Disabilities*, Gloucester, MA: People with Disabilities Press, 2002.

Robert Osgood, *The History of Inclusion in the United States.*, Washington, DC: Gallaudet University Press, 2005.

Erik Parens and Adrienne Asch, eds., *Prenatal Testing and Disability Rights*, Washington, DC: Georgetown University Press, 2000.

Philip L. Safford and Elizabeth J. Safford, *Children with Disabilities in America: A Historical Handbook and Guide*, Westport, CT: Greenwood, 2006.

Joseph P. Shapiro, *No Pity: People with Disabilities Forging a New Civil Rights Movement*, New York: Random House, 1993.

Duane F. Stroman, *The Disability Rights Movement: From Deinstitutionalization to Self-Determination*, Lanham, MD: University Press of America, 2003.

David Wasserman, Jerome Bickenbach, Robert Wachbroit, eds., *Quality of Life and Human Difference: Genetic Testing, Health Care, and Disability (Cambridge Studies in Philosophy and Public Policy)*, Cambridge, UK: Cambridge University Press, 2005.

Periodicals

Charlotte Allen, "Identity Politics Gone Wild: The Deaf Culture Wars at Gallaudet University," *The Weekly Standard*, April 2, 2007.

Lee Benson, "Disability Doesn't Limit Lover of Life," *Deseret Morning News*, February 20, 2008.

Frank Bowe, "Disability Meets the Boom," *Ragged Edge*, September 27, 2005.

Lynne Brown, "Enabling Disabled Shoppers," *Internet Retailer*, January 2008.

Ruth Colker, "The Mythic 43 Million Americans with Disabilities," *William and Mary Law Review*, October 1, 2007.

Gretchen Cook, "Siblings of Disabled Have Their Own Troubles," *New York Times*, April 3, 2006.

Digital Solidarity, "Interview: Down Syndrome Is Not a Disease, But Another Personal Characteristic," *Disability World*, June–August 2002.

Stephen Gold, "Beyond Pity and Paternalism," *The Other Side*, September 1, 2002.

Amy Harmon, "Prenatal Test Puts Down Syndrome in Hard Focus," *New York Times*, May 9, 2007.

Janine Manny, "Labor of Love: Disabled Woman Finds Dream Job in Ttutoring Program," *Daily News Online*, October 1, 2007.

Harriet McBryde Johnson, "Unspeakable Conversations," *New York Times Magazine*, February 16, 2003.

Sue Anne Pressley Montes, "Opening the Door to Independent Living," *Washington Post*, March 8, 2008.

David Mortimer, "New Eugenics and the Newborn: The Historical 'Cousinage' of Eugenics and Infanticide," *Ethics & Medicine*, Fall 2003.

Corbett Joan O'Toole, "1981–2002: How Women with Disabilities Have Changed the World," *off our backs*, January/February 2003.

Rick Rader, "Like Pearls, They Need to Be Strung Together," *The Exceptional Parent*(Boston), June 2007.

Marta Russell, "Targeting Disability," *Monthly Review*, April 2005.

Michael J. Sandel, "What's Wrong with Designer Children, Bionic Athletes, and Genetic Engineering?" *Atlantic Monthly* April 2004.

Julian Savulescu, "Resources, Down's Syndrome, and Cardiac Surgery," *British Medical Journal*, April 14, 2001.

Bobby Schindler, "Since When Does Pro-Life Mean Killing the Disabled?" *Dakota Voice*, May 9, 2007.

Susan Ann Silverstein, "Human Rights Heroes," *Human Rights* (Chicago), July 2007.

Robert Tomsho, "The Special-Education Debate—Is Main-streaming Good or Bad for Kids?" *Baltimore Sun*, November 27, 2007.

Web Sites

Americans with Disabilities Act Document Center, www.jan.wvu.edu/links/adalinks.htm

Department of Justice ADA, www.usdoj.gov/crt/ada

Disabilities History Museum, www.disabilitymuseum.org

DisabilityInfo.gov, www.disabilityInfo.gov

Disability Social History Project, www.disabilityhistory.org

Disability Statistics Center, www.dsc.ucsf.edu/main.php

Disabled World, www.disabled-world.com

Kids Together, Inc., www.kidstogether.org

Index

A

Abortion, 178
Access, 48–53
Activism, 17, 20, 59, 172
Adaptive technology, 54–57
    Dragon Naturally Speaking, 55
    Jaws, 55
    Kurzweil 3000, 57
    Zoomtext, 55
Adaptive Technology Center (ATC), 54
Alliance for Full Participation in America, 68
American Association on Mental Retardation (AAMR), 68, 97
American Medical Directors Association, 61
American Psychiatric Association, 97
American Psychological Association, 105
American Sign Language, 156
Americans with Disabilities Act (ADA), 18, 60, 79–83, 132
    benefits, 84–85
    case law, 88–89
    civic participation, 52
    civil rights, 52
    deficiencies, 84–85
    discrimination, 50–51
    economic access, 53
    effects, 52–53
    elements, 51
    employment, 85
    goals, 50–51
    impact, 82–83
    legal enforcement, 51–52
    progress, 48
    public access, 51
    rationale, 79
    reasonable accommodation, 48
    scope, 81
    shortcomings, 84, 87
    social access, 51
ARC (National Association for Retarded Children), 17, 60
Arc of Northern Virginia, 65
Arc of the United States, 68
Archives of Pediatrics and Adolescent Medicine (journal), 167
Asch, Adrienne, 172
The Ashley Treatment, 163
Associated Press, 167
ATC (Adaptive Technology Center), 54
Atkins v. Virginia, 96–98
Audiology Online, 150
Autism, 117, 133
Autism Research Institute, 71
Axis II disorders, 104

B

Bell, Alexander Graham, 157
Bender, Joyce, 86
Best Buddies, 120–123
Binet Simon (intelligence test), 99
Bio-conservatives, 171
Bioethics, 171
Blindness, 54
The Board of Education v. Mills, 131
Boccelli, Andrea, 162
Bollinger, Allen, 22